PSYCHOTHERAPY

Dialogue with the Late Alexander McQueen

BOOK ONE

By Apple Dasorine

DISCLAIMER

This book is not intended as a substitute for the medical advice of physicians. The reader should regularly consult a physician in matters relating to his/her health and particularly with respect to any symptoms that may require diagnosis or medical attention.

Although the author and publisher have made every effort to ensure that the information in this book was correct at press time, the author and publisher do not assume and hereby disclaim any liability to any party for any loss, damage, or disruption caused by errors or omissions, whether such errors or omissions result from negligence, accident, or any other cause.

PUBLISHER"S CONTACT INFORMATION

For readers who have questions or might be interested in reporting an error they find in the book.

Apple Dasorine
3107-13827 100th Ave
Surrey, BC
Canada
V3T 5L2

appledasorine.com

In dedication to Will & Stefani,

In saving humanity as one,

You are still my golden rainbow.

Beyond the Skull

It formed thick obsidian,

Flaming fire turned frost,

Scales slithering,

Deep eyes of needle hole slits,

Robbed by golden poverty,

Swallowing their sharp fish bones,

Raped by shards of glass,

Screaming no echo,

Undressing fabrics of insane,

Gasoline tears bled inside,

Smoke a bottomless fog,

Vacuumed in cutting light,

Hear ye cry,

Feel ye pain,

Arrive,

Mend ye stolen breath,

Without bones and skull.

- The Late Lee McQueen

PREFACE

I have pre-written this as a journal which was the rough draft of the dialogue between Alexander McQueen and I through automatic writing. I have rewrote the journal as a short memoir in a form of my own healing and guidance finding my true calling associated with my beliefs as a Wiccan. I state every part of the writing are 100% true and I am sorry for those offended by any of the events occurred or some of explicit language used.

I understand the consequences of publishing writings of a high profile person but his wishes are to have me produce this for his own reasons. The main reasons are in relation of curing chronic depression, mental illness and the invisible forces that are harmful to the human race. We have meant no harm in the production of this book and hope it's a useful tool for people struggling with trauma and the unexplained.

I am not an experienced writer and I get to the point without the sugarcoating. I hope that by releasing from my heart I can inspire others to come forward with their own stories to help us heal as a whole. I have shed many tears by writing this book. The magic of understanding the insanity of dysfunction can help us towards brightening our era of new age by opening our minds. Thank you to all readers for purchasing my book. Please read along with an open mind, loving, respect and kindness.

I

THE VEIL

During many months of self-loathing loneliness, I have slipped myself deep into the unknown. Through mindfulness mediation and chakra balancing, I tried to look for clarity behind my depressive state and the traumatic cycles in my life.

I dedicated my life to treating others with respect, done things the right way and never intentionally hurt anyone. I have always followed the inspirational teachings of Jesus, Buddha, Mohammad and others. Their essence in their wisdom delivered such great messages to human kind since our longevity of our existence. The roots of all their teachings delivered great messages to humanity. I have always found each spiritual practice uniquely precious leading and transforming human behavior back to the magnificent Godhead.

I have always thanked the Higher Power and had gratitude towards my life during the glorious and the atrocious times. I tried releasing my sadness, my pain and fears to God. However, often I have wondered why I feel my soul nailed to a flaming crucifix. Why does my subconscious mind bleed so many tears? It's become a curse of my inherited dysfunction.

My Thai roots growing up was to follow the Buddhist teachings of the Noble Eight Fold Path: Right Speech, Right Action, Right Livelihood, Right Effort, Right Mindfulness, and Right Concentration. I feel that by even practicing this, I am guided back to a position of torment where my chakras were charred. Why must I feel this way? Why must I endure so much persecution?

My gleaming light and attitude for life has become a thunderous gloom. My dreams and reality became a repeating cinema of cycles of treacherous experiences. I have searched several spiritual teachings to release the thoughts of my misery and demons behind the sharp wounds embedded in my existence.

Homeless and lonely, I have surrounded myself of the things that I once treasured and have forgotten. A bookcase tells me a story of my past that I have tried to bury in the black hole of my subconscious. Books of religion, philosophy, spiritual teachings, the magical mystics and the books that haunt me the most, fashion.

A statue of a Buddha sitting under a small pillow guards the fifth shelf where a vase of precious crow feathers pose. Each one reminds me of sunny walks alone associating each one with a message from the divine. I carried each one with honor and collected hundreds throughout the years until my belongings were separated by heart wrenching divorce.

I transformed this room into a cave of artistic production to clear my mind. My mystical paintings filled the walls. The corner under the unused fireplace show a collection of colorful paints and paint brushes I once joyfully used. Beside that is a collection of sculptures neglected when having experimented with clay is what I see sitting on that cold leather futon. For months, I haven't acknowledged to call this my home, neglected to call that futon my bed.

Being unemployed has made me lose the reality of time. Sleeping in the middle of the morning into the late afternoon sunset. I drink when thirsty, eat when hungry, shower if I have to leave the house and connect with friends if necessary. There is no schedule, no cycle of the mechanical life I once had. I just have, me, myself and I searching for ways to repair my life.

In the dim candle lit room after my mindfulness meditation, I felt like breaking down not receiving any answers or feeling like any of my pain has released. I never felt so much twilight looking for guidance to heal myself. As I got off the white plush rug and stepped three steps away on to the futon, I thought maybe I should journal my thoughts again. Beside me I grabbed a notepad and a pen to write once again.

Then the unexpected happened, a British voice that spoken of Alexander McQueen tells me to journal him and everything we talk about. Concerned about my mental state and in disbelief, I still started to write.

Me: Why can I hear you so clearly? Before you were just in my subconscious but now you are actually wanting a communication.

McQueen: I am here now when you need me the most, at your lowest. You have given up on fashion, a part of yourself and I am here to teach you and guide you how important it is to keep your fashion roots through your darkest hour. Through fashion you can heal through this.

All I am thinking at this point is that I am going crazy. I thought of all those chakra meditations that could if helped me discover and open my third eye. For years I was searching for a connection with the divine, something magical but certainly not the spirit of the late Alexander McQueen!

Me: I am not going crazy right? Please tell me I am not insane!

McQueen: You knew you were always nonhuman. You knew deep inside of you that you have a strong connection of both the Ethereal and Inferno. You are a lot like me finding beauty in both worlds. But right now you need me the most. You are losing yourself to this dimension.

Me: Well, I have lost everything! My business, the man I love, my personal belongings and my home. I live in my mother's living room for God sake! I am thirty-five years old with nine dollars in my bank account and at my lowest I have ever been.

At this moment I felt a fire bursting throughout my aura. The madness of everything I had to endure that took me to this point. Fashion was something I wanted to leave in the grave. Every time I thought of it, or saw it, I just wanted to cease to exist in my life.

McQueen: Beauty is in the lowest places. I am here to remind you of it. Without seeing things at this prospective, you cannot see the inner essence in all your other successes you have achieved and the inner riches it has brought you. Being rich is not your bank account, it's how your knowledge can influence the world. I know this and been where you are.

Me: For such a successful person, I would expect you to be in the fashion world with your creative team channeling ideas for them. Why are you here?

I thought the spirit of Alexander McQueen would be more involved with creating marvelous designs for his fashion house. I thought he be in more important places in the world than be here with me. I mean, what did I mean to him? I never met this guy before in my life and only saw two of his fashion shows. He's not even my favorite fashion designer.

McQueen: I have always been here with you, Apple. I have always tried to get your attention. I influenced you to take Fashion Merchandising. I was with you in class helping you through projects. You always knew I was there but you ignored me because you were afraid to speak up. Yes, I was a successful fashion designer in my life but now I am just a spirit of one. I take a different role as a spirit but it's still my influence from beyond the grave.

Now I was placing the broken puzzle pieces together. There was a time when I had to make a choice of either Makeup Artistry or Fashion Merchandising.

Something did nudge me to be in the Fashion Industry. I was more curious now because there were times I thought about Alexander McQueen as a lonely fashion designer that lost touch with reality. I had asked God why this happens to people. I had my own thoughts towards suicide, something I never have the guts to do but can feel why people would lose themselves to it.

Me: How long have you been watching me?

McQueen: The afterlife has no concept of time. I was always one of your Spirit Guides in spirit form. I am in your life blueprint as only a spirit because you don't care for celebrity status or the celebrity world. That's why in school you were even afraid to utter my fashion label. You said your favorite designer was John Galliano when everyone else praised my work. In your heart, if you had millions of dollars, you would wear couture every day. Where you live, people are so casual it lost the fashionable side of you even so when you started working in Formal Menswear. You hid your couture side inside the bridal industry because that's where it was the most couture it got where you live.

My thoughts were turning at this time. I did understand the cycle of life beyond the Earth form. I have studied this and analyzed this before. Before this conversation, I have looked into who my Spirit Guides were and how to connect with them. I heard once that one of them was Quan Yin, the Chinese Goddess of Compassion but never believed it because that person maybe associated her with me because of my Asian ethnicity. I never thought that a fashion designer would ever connect with me and tell me all this. No one really knew I secretly love John Galliano's work or that I would wear couture every day. I hated fashion and where it's taken me today. Thinking of the stresses of it, I never wanted to return to such a vain, materialistic industry.

Me: I can't even look at a suit or tuxedo without tearing up. It's traumatizing right now. I spent a large portion of my life to learn fashion, tailoring and styling menswear and lost everything doing it. It's been eight months since losing my shop and I haven't even said a word to part of my creative team I was working with. The lost love of my life spent over $100,000 on my big *dreams to come true and I lost it all. And I ask for what?*

McQueen: Failure is about learning. You have forgot to learn and move on. That experience made you grow. That path was not for you. You were stuck in that bloody shop for sixty hours a week and working from home. You lost yourself pleasing others then you noticed those people got pickier, it was never enough. You let your clients step all over you. They abused your kindness and the support you needed was also injected by fear. The boss and mentor who sold you his shop was somewhat jealous and still needed to feel superior because he failed in there so you were playing tug a war. He felt if you made more money in there than him, you shouldn't be more than him. It was pride. He couldn't see you succeed because it would if killed him and now he had to live through shutting it down. It was nothing that you did. It was you trying to take something that was broken and stitching the pieces back together when the thread was too thin and the needle was too dull.

For the several years I worked with Won, we always had a brother-sister relationship. I learned so many lessons working with him but it was like nothing was good enough especially for the clients in that demographic. Won taught me some operational and management skills in that Tuxedo Rental Shop enough for me to eventually move on and learn how to customize suits in menswear. I searched for profitable quality suppliers overseas for months and the one manufacture I was working with first, Won eventually stole and started outsourcing from them first. The first wedding contract for six tuxedo rentals I had after buying out his shop, he took away the ties and shoes and I was asked to pay extra for them. The bride was so upset that during their tuxedo fitting, there were no ties or shoes when I had promised the whole package. During the several months, Won would call me to ask how things were only to give me a cruel lecture where hanging up would lead me to tears. I just wanted it to all disappear! Everything fashion, just go.

McQueen: I saw that. Also every time your joy and light came back designing for a client, he would dim your light and that energy would bring you negative results in the ordering process. Mistakes were made in the other end and you lost more money getting garments tailored. Outsourcing for you was a bit of a nightmare but also you high super high bills you couldn't reach every month. I am here to say it was not your fault. You worked the hardest to please people with swords stuck on your back. The sorrow and the pain you experience at this moment is lifting each sword off. Every time you feel like crying, remember a sword is being carefully removed and the wounds are being healed.

I recognized all the strain and torture that shop brought me but the suffering of it still lingered. The bills were so awful that Will and I were fighting more and started neglecting each other. I spent more time trying to become successful for him to be proud that we made it in business together. I only wished that it never happened, then we would if never got divorced. It was all in guilty pleasure, wanting more when we already had more than enough.

Me: I never wanted to be associated with depression but yesterday was my all-time lowest. The tears won't come anymore but it's now wounded so deep that light cannot even touch it.

McQueen: If it's so dark, seek the beauty within it and appreciate it. The problem with you is that you try to seek light into everything and when it is dark, you get depressed because it stays that way. There's no light in it, it's just the way it is. Seek beauty in it. In other words, fur cannot become silk. They are separate entities.

Beauty within darkness I have understood this but I try to see the light in everything. Maybe Won was there to push me? Maybe there was a good conclusion in owning that store that never succeeded? It's just bullshit, all of it.

Me: But then you are feeling darkness? How does that make sense?

McQueen: You are not feeling it. You are just to letting it be. On your dimension, you are lucky to experience both light and darkness and turn it into a creation. The afterlife's dimension is much different. We see creation from the beginning to end and work for the enhancement of spirit where on your dimension it's simply for humanity. In humanity, they care about beautiful materialistic things because you can touch it, wear it and makes you feel a certain way where in my dimension we think of it and it's just there, no feelings attached. Time is crucial to humans as there is a beauty to building. I am here with you because throughout your life, you have a lot of darkness. People look at you and don't see any trauma. People misjudge you because you are pretty. Just like the models I have worked with they all had struggles just to get on that runway. You think being pretty is a curse but others think it's a blessing. On Earth, it's called polarizing when everything has an opposite. You have always known this truth as a Wiccan.

At this point, I knew he was right. That it could be a great thing to create something magical and inspire others with. With the bulk of my problems, I didn't see how. I really saw no way out with nine dollars in my bank account without a home or a job. I did understand the other dimensions and how it translates into a magnificent cycle back to the unity of the Godhead. But here on Earth, it's like a rebirth of suffering every day. I mean, why me and why do I go through all this distress? Even with my looks, I still get so many negative judgments. I just can't win.

Me: Yes, but I have struggled to own it in my life. Because the situations are very dark and then I am judged by my looks. They didn't like me fat and ugly and now they don't like me fit and attractive.

McQueen: Let's move forward and talk about each sword being removed and I will help you love fashion out of this depression.

The pen suddenly stood still and his voice disappeared into the abyss. I still don't understand why his spirit was here with me. I often had pleasures invoking other entities like Angels or Demons being Wiccan. It was truly something I understood becoming more involved with magic and being a Spiritualist.

The past I was trying to bury was my love of creating a fashion career. I was fighting two separate entities. How does spirituality blend with fashion? How could I balance the two and mesh them together? That was my old world in that lonely shop fighting to keep my clients, struggling to keep Won content and being a good house wife to Will, I eventually broke down.

I hated my past, tried to escape it but it kept coming back. Was McQueen really trying to help me? Was it really him? I was skeptical. But at this moment I thought even if it wasn't him, it might help me through all of this. I need to give him a chance. Maybe he's trying to make up for leaving his life the way he did leaving everything behind.

At one point I thought about where souls go after they committed suicide. My mother and father being Buddhists say they don't go to a good place and that they need to relive that day over and over again until their rightful time in old age or sickness has come. I read that there are two places they can go, to the left door turning away from the Godhead or to the white light. Some souls I heard are ashamed of the Godhead or being judged so they pick the left door where their lost souls wonder around in darkness. Some souls may be attached to their personal belongings or a person, this one we call ghosts.

I believe that if they picked the white light to the Godhead, they dance in the perfect bliss of love where friends and family members that have deceased welcome them to the Afterlife. If there were souls that had bad trauma, they would send them into a cocoon of twilight sleep filled with blissful love in order to restore the pure essence of their soul in the Ethereal dimension.

I believe that there isn't a right or wrong way and that everything we document has a special story to inspire and restore humanity. I believe that maybe McQueen also has a story to tell given that I know nothing about him but only giving him sympathy becoming lost in this world. I remember hearing that the veil was beginning to open. The veil between us and the Ethereal. If so, that means the veil of the Inferno also has been opened because everything does have an opposite.

This may be a scary thought to believers of many religions but I have never been afraid. The existence of a Hell means that those creatures, thoughts of evil and the malevolent stay there and isn't leaked into the Ethereal. Sometimes with our man-made thoughts we create madness and a Hell on Earth with war and famine.

Hopefully the veil can be lifted to help us as a whole to create a good change in our world. This conversation with McQueen can maybe help me, I don't know. I have nothing to lose and everything to gain from listening. I am not sure about the whole fashion thing, I have already given it my all.

I turn around and look at the time. It's 4am and I need to rest. I've already calculated that I'll be tossing and turning for another hour before actually sleeping. I'll be waking up in the afternoon facing another secluded unmotivated day taking care of my sick grandmother who lives in the next room. I lean over to snuff two candles out with a glass jar, put away my pad and paper and tuck in for the lonely night.

II

PUPPET

I had left the house for two days feeling run down. My eyes were puffy and I was afraid people would see me in knots. I didn't feel like myself or a sense of belonging. I once cherished a picket fence life for myself, a traditional life. Social media surrounded me with acquaintances with cheerful pictures capturing joyful family gatherings, weddings and newborns. I felt like everyone was enjoying a perfect life except for me. What was wrong with me? Why don't I deserve such a life?

I heard once before that whatever your life is at the moment is what you brought to yourself. I heard that whatever you have you deserve. Opening the glass balcony door, pulling away the fleshy cotton curtains, I looked forward to the possessions I was left with. A cold leather futon sits in the middle of the wooden floor. It's where my cinema of decayed thoughts and nightmares take place.

I slide off the rain boots borrowed from my niece and take off my military wool jacket hanging it on the bamboo chair I turned into a clothing pile. To the left of that is a wardrobe filled with second hand clothing and some pieces I bought from my devastating trip to Thailand two months ago. I only carried 5% of my old precious wardrobe. It depressed me more thinking about the garments that I once wore with pride.

I look down at my paints and the sculptures I was experimenting with. My inspiration to create had vanished and all I had was heartless thoughts. I had always been a loving, kind and caring person but this is what I deserve. I deserve to be alone living with only pieces of myself. He took everything away from me and he rewards me with broken tears. I still don't understand why I try to patch up the crumbled pieces. I had sacrificed my well-being just to feel love but with that so much pain.

I hate what I have become. I became surrounded with seclusion and the delusion to look perfect, be happy, and just enjoy life. The life that I once had filled me with inspiration and once promised me with a great future. In one day, I watched that life flicker and burn with moist eyes. The thriving pulse I had for life turned into a lifeless coma. The reality of malevolent beings crept in my thoughts. I have always been living the angelic way all my life but still suffer in torment. What lessons was I learning? Which Godhead would make me endure such pain?

I had no way of knowing how to release this. No friend or family member could understand what I have become. I plop myself on the futon thinking, there must be a way. Across from me was a leather trunk with my incense, candles and bundles of sage. I light a black candle to get rid of negativity and burned an incense between my fingers in prayer. As the room of smoke filled with myrrh, he came back. I quickly grasped my pen and paper.

McQueen: You were crying so hard last night. I felt the sadness, the same feeling when Isabella left. Let's release this.

Me: It's an emotional relationship that used to be an engagement together three years. Before losing the shop, I was coping with his alcohol abuse and my own perfection to be successful. I was hard on myself and he was hard on me as he was paying for all the bills. Our gas got cut off and there was no hot water running in our home. I just broke down. Now at this moment, I just see a black cloud hovering over our future. Who is Isabella?

I felt that no one understood me and that I had no ear but him to talk to at this point. There's no human out there that can relate to the loss I submitted to. It was almost embarrassing to let people know I was seeing Will again after what he did to me. I feared the people that I once called family would judge me for being so weak. How could you let him damage you over and over again and why was I was attached to it? The cycle was sick but I only loved him so much.

McQueen: She was a long-time beloved friend of mine who was also my fashion stylist before my fame and during the middle of my career. She was with me from the beginning and she committed suicide three years before my death. She had a lot to do with the creativity behind the brand. When she died, I blamed myself and it always stuck by me until my death. I later saw that I had abandoned her before her death. The rise of my brand had an effect on everyone that was loyal to me from the beginning.

Me: I had no idea.

McQueen: If I had to do it all over again, I would if saved her. When I took my own life, I felt like I needed to be with her too. To mend the pain. The fame was no longer happiness without my number one fans including my mother. You have lost someone due to suicide too I gather.

I wheeled in my mind how he got this information that I held so secretly but he is a Spirit Guide isn't he? For twenty years, I have not expressed her to anyone but my family. It was a devastating episode that shook the way I viewed how life and death was supposed to be. It made me search for answers to what happens after death. Being so young back then, I only thought of Heaven and Hell.

Me: Yes, my stepmother, Carol-Lee. When I was fifteen, she made me a gin and tonic on a school night and we were talking and smoking cigarettes in my room. She was a cool stepmom.. I was so tired and she was so drunk while I fell asleep. Then at 7am, a police officer woke me up and told me come downstairs as he had something to tell us. I saw my brother and sister run down the stairs to hear what had happened. They told us that she shot herself in the head in her closet.

McQueen: At fifteen, what were your memories of her?

I had to dig out a buried shelf in my subconscious. The faint memories I had of her were somewhat inspirational but at the same time damaging.

Me: She was half Indigenous with big brown eyes and puffed hair that covered half of her back. She was kind and always thought of the kids before herself. I had a good connection with her and had many good conversations. She was the first one that introduced me to the occult. I was taught how to properly use the Ouija Board by her and made my first board. I had promised her that if she died that I would contact her through the board which I did later in life. I was a troubled teenager, smoking weed, skipping school and shoplifting. She would always try to find ways to punish me and even talked about sending me off to boarding school.

My first contact with the Ouija Board was the most exciting tool I ever used to communicate with spirits. She had test questions I had to seek of her deceased cousin. I remembered gathering all that information from the Ouija Board while each correct answer proved that I was in contact with her. After Carol-Lee died, I never thought about using the Ouija Board much but thought of other methods to communicate with the dead.

McQueen: She wanted you to learn fashion, didn't she?

I quickly turned to anger and hated myself for what fashion has done to me. Words floated around my head. Judgmental. Materialistic. Vanity. Useless. If I knew I was going to be in this position, I would if never considered fashion to be part of my life.

Me: Yes, but she's dead. In the grave like fashion.

McQueen: It's the cycle of life and death. Romantic isn't it? There's a reason why she gave you that message. You will understand why soon and how it all comes together. When you were fifteen, my collection "La Poupee" was being presented. It means "The Doll" in French. We used the vision of distorted toy dolls to experiment the limits of proportion using water as an element of the runway. I had Kate expose part of her bum for my iconic bumster pants.

Okay, call me crazy but I had no idea he created "Bumster Pants". I actually didn't really pay attention to anything McQueen because it was so mainstream. I mean, everyone loved his work. I only watched maybe two shows of his at the most because of my classes in Fashion Merchandising but he wasn't my ideal designer.

Me: Why would you create such a weird pant?

McQueen: Nothing in fashion is weird. It's all an expression, Apple! Look at it this way, the bottom part of the spine is the most erotic, seductive and sensual part of the body no matter what gender you are. I was thinking to elongate and extend the body so I created a new contour on the buttocks and that's how the bumster was created a couple years before this one.

Okay, now I had to see this. I grabbed my laptop under the futon and opened the bright screen. I haven't watched a woman's runway show in years. Most of my fashion work was all in menswear. I didn't have time to care for runway shows, fashion blogs or fashion magazines. I always was a hermit wanting to be independent in my career and have a loving marriage. I wanted nothing more. The thought of even looking for this fashion show took a lot of courage. I secretly despised myself for it.

The show was not what I expected. It was unique to see the runway filled with water, nudity was certainly visible and there was a model attached to metal bars wearing a mesh, fringed dress. It was kind of creepy to see her tied up in a square cage dancing inside like a trance. It reminded me of slaving away to society. It reminded me of myself and what I really walked like.

McQueen: It was a good show. The great times with my original team.

Me: This show was somewhat galactic and was like you were way ahead of your time. There is quite a lot of nudity as well. How was the reaction of your critics?

McQueen: I never cared what people thought really. There were so many different reactions even though the show was well liked, it did create a buzz. I wanted to keep pushing my limits. I wanted to be the star of the unimaginable.

Me: The bumster pants actually wasn't that shocking. Right now people would consider a low cut trouser. I see where it comes from now.

Overall, the show was very theatrical, almost like there was a hidden message. Was there something McQueen want to unleash? Was there a cryptic message hidden in this shows? He was very talented creating lovely textures and diverse silhouettes. He was kind of a fashion scientist if there was one.

McQueen: Kate was so brilliant and vibrant to me and was a tremendous success to have her wear them.

Me: I must say, the show was like a performance. A fashionably lit play with exciting artistic garments.

McQueen: Fashion was very different back then. The boundaries were limitless and the performances were more theatrical.

Me: Your tailoring I must say was quite impeccable.

There were some pieces of fine tailoring that I didn't expect. I didn't even know that McQueen was into tailoring. From the previous shows I watched of him, it was more dresses. I thought that was his specialty.

McQueen: I knew you would love the tailoring. That is something we both share in common.

Me: I can't believe I was only fifteen when this was shown. I never even knew you were designing until I watched your documentary in 2010. I was quite amazed at your success back then but also felt your sadness due to your suicide. I think it really related that to Carol-Lee. She always told me to be in the fashion industry because I was quite different and more fashionable than others.

McQueen: I was there in spirit. You moved back to the city and then enrolled in school. I nudged your decision for Fashion Merchandising. You have always channeled me.

I remember living on the island, a two hour ferry ride away from the city. It was one of the first times I ever felt sadness from a spirit. I didn't know how it was exactly but I was laying on the couch with the sun beaming on my face when a chill blew across my lips and felt like I was going to cry for no reason. I had my eyes closed and I just broke down in tears. It wasn't me, it was the unknown.

I heard his voice before but ignored it, closing the veil. I didn't want people to think I was crazy, I didn't want them to know I was even hearing voices. I had to learn the hard way that I was a Trance Medium. I had to except something I didn't know how to explain or grasp.

Me: In class, I knew that but it was very hard to explain. I thought I was crazy in a way. How do you explain that one of the most talented designers ever lived to be channeled through me?

McQueen: People are hesitant to trust their own gut so don't ever be afraid to express yourself.

Me: So what is your purpose now?

McQueen: To end your depression through the love of fashion. Not only through fashion, but through the things you love. You have always wanted to do something good for humanity. Through your own pain and suffering, there is a part me that needs to be expressed. Fashion is a medium and is embedded a religion to me and need to help others find and express theirs.

I once had a way to express myself. I had painting, sculpting, drawing and writing. I didn't think I was good at any of those things but only used them for an outlet. Almost like artistic therapy because I was a monster. It was hard to connect with people the way I was supposed to. I wasn't into social media and socializing. It only made me take on their issues emotionally. My problems were more severe and I felt guilty for disconnecting and self-loathing.

Me: So you were depressed too in some stages in your life?

McQueen: I suffered from chronic depression but hid it in my work. After my death, I realized that it was a lonely road and I was also dealing with the suffering of a past life. It was a door that had not closed. I was yearning and seeking for that without knowing. It was all through my work and you will see this. When my mother died, it struck me hard. I couldn't continue without her cheering me on. Just like Isabella, I couldn't lose another.

I knew what he went through was painful but I knew where his spirit was now. A divine place abundant of pure love. I've heard this many times before when you cross over and go towards the light, you end up there. If he was willing to help me, what for and why me?

Me: So do you think communicating this now and helping me out of depression will make up for your death?

McQueen: It is my path. To help stop that feeling, that feeling of giving it up and ending it all.

Dealing with Carol-Lee's suicide, I never considered taking my own life. I would feel more remorse watching the people around me in sadness because of losing me. At this point I thought I don't have anything to lose anyway. I mean, a lot of things I mostly loved and cherished has been stolen away from me and no one to blame but myself. Suicide was never an answer even though it has been a brutal road.

Me: I can relate. I never had suicidal thoughts because I simply do not have the guts to end my life. My feelings are just low-spirited, dejection and extreme sadness.

McQueen: Your life has had extreme trauma and every single ordeal, there was no release or outlet. Yesterday you pulled out a sword on your back. That one was called "expectation".

I gave it a minute and thought of my old routines and how I used to live my life. Maybe it wasn't supposed to be the life for me but still, I was searching for my happiness.

Me: I clearly understand. I thought getting back together with Will everything would be the same. Living apart seems so distant and it's been challenging because we have never done this before. It's like a separation and being secluded all the time. My eyes did clear up now and I see it is a smart choice by taking things slow and see where it takes us. He is still an alcoholic and that is an emotional baggage to carry. His priorities are not us and soon I may have to change my priorities to unleash my true potential.

McQueen: In your dimension, nothing and nobody is ever perfect. It does make things phenomenal because where I am, creation is lifeless. There is an enormous deal being human and being able to invent for human life which is where I see my absence. I have inspired many people but my own demons took a hold of me.

I knew what he meant. There are so many famous artists that take their own lives. There is definitely a sufficient sadness most successful artists feel when they are on this dimension. Even though their creative ideas spread to millions worldwide, there is still this complete emptiness. I had to find out the reason for this. How do you stop extreme sadness?

Me: You were a legendary artist not only an infamous fashion designer but quite an influential person as well.

McQueen: I was confused at what I wanted. I wanted to be a fashion designer exploring limits and breaking rules but I did not expect the fame. I wanted people to know who I was, not just my performances. My life became me being a fashion machine performing and producing. Once that happened, I lost the people that meant the most to me and I was broken. It wasn't so fun anymore. I thought what was I doing all this for?

Almost like how I felt working at my shop but the opposite. I felt failure where he had success. He was alone but I was married ending up in divorce. I lost a Carol-Lee due to suicide and he lost himself.

Me: You were doing it for humanity and it was not only in your designs. It was your attitude about it. To be yourself and stay unique.

McQueen: I know my lessons now. After my death, I have learned all the pieces to the puzzle. Now I need for you to understand what you are and want you to take my influence and be yourself as unique as you are. You are quite an interesting person.

Me: It's been hard for me to translate what I am and what I know. Then I go through these weird emotions that are not even my own. Some people have told me that I was not human and I have searched my whole life to seek what I truly am.

The pen stopped writing again and he was gone. Alone again where are we going with this? His spirit was better than none so I have accepted him to communicate with me. Maybe I can finally find pieces hidden in myself. Maybe it can help me explore my happiness again.

That scene of that model dancing in that caged dress made me think. How could that linger in a mind of someone? It was something out of a horror show. It did however bring me back feelings of being strapped to my dysfunction, my depression. That was a clear vision of what it looked like.

Was McQueen in fact invoking something through his work? Why did he vividly have visions of the Inferno and why was he so curious of the Afterlife? That was the first show I have seen of his that was vintage. I never seen anything like it and had the shock value throughout. It's completely dark but appreciative even though the clothes were unwearable. It tells a story, a journal of insanity living in his mind. It reminds me of my mind.

Whatever it is it was all part of creation. It's something he's trying to translate for me. I have always believed that God has created us to reflect parts of himself. Images that are beautifully perfect in every each way. By saying this, are we puppets? Is there something beyond that control our thoughts and actions?

My eyes were still puffy after crying for two hours the night before. I didn't feel like cleansing myself which was abnormal. I didn't feel like meditating either. I just wanted to be alone at peace and just forget the hurt that I was getting used to. My love wasn't perfection anymore, it was a cycle of pain. What did we do to each other and how did it end up like this?

I am truly a monster. Not a soul would understand what the hell I am. I don't even understand myself! I have pure kindness in my thoughts with humanity but when I am alone, it's as if I am fuming with hatred with sorrow and mindfulness disabilities. I can't stand to live this way anymore. I need to find an outlet.

III

SIAM

I finally woke up to a mindless thick fog. I turn my head to face the time on the digital radio clock and its 4:32pm. I have wasted my whole day but what was the point to get up earlier? What should I be doing? It's not like I had a job or friends to see. I was okay with being secluded now. It was safe.

I make myself a cup of coffee and walked five steps to the balcony and light a smoke. I saw that people were returning from their daily responsibilities. Must be nice to have something to look forward to. Going to school or having a job, is this what life is about? I take an inhale and exhale and felt a mind numb. First smoke of the day, it's the only time I could feel my brain buzz.

I slip back into the room and look at my phone only to see the reflection of myself. Then I reminisced a dream I had last night. I was with McQueen in the Ethereal looking down at the Inferno. We were sitting on a cloud and he told me to look for him in the underworld.

Looking down, I saw various malevolent beings with giant wings. Gruesome monsters with more than one head and demonic figures that looked like giant insects with beady red eyes. They were surrounded in a cave of fire and a lakes of blood and human organs. I heard screams that echoed through the eyes of the hellish beings.

I saw him chained to a monstrous being. It was as high as a three story building with wrinkly scaly skin and eyes like a reptilian. It looked like he was torturing him pushing his face into what looked like flaming lava. He wasn't screaming even though his face distorted.

On the cloud he was still beside me. I asked, why he was there and beside me at the same time. He answered, "That was how I felt at the state of my depression on Earth. It stays in the Inferno and I sit here looking down at it as it stays down untouched by the Ethereal."

That's all I could remember from that chilly nightmare. All I could think of is I've been tapping into too many third eye meditations opening up dimensions I couldn't explain. Maybe it was just a dream letting go parts of my subconscious. Whatever it was, it really didn't make me feel any better.

I heard a door open across from me and peeping out is my sick grandmother. I look at her and think of how lonely she is without much care outside of myself. I have accidentally became a care-aid cooking, cleaning and translating her doctor appointments. I didn't sign up for this assignment but I am here for reason. I have took on this responsibility on behalf of my workaholic mother but what they don't know is that I am secretly fighting myself and my own health and sanity.

She walks two steps to get to the bathroom to clean up and I thought that I had some time to kill before showering. Then the spirit of McQueen came back again. I launch out my notepad and pen as he began to speak.

McQueen: You have been oversleeping lately.

Me: I don't know what's wrong with me. I feel my body needs it but it's like my whole day has vanished.

McQueen: You are a night owl and need to dream to release tension. You may have bad dreams but it's for you to release your fears subconsciously.

How the hell did he know about my dreams? I was wondering if he could also hear my thoughts as well. Releasing my fears made sense but I have already made that my reality. I have lost everything based on fear. I foresaw I was going to become homeless and Will was going to abandon me. Now I have to live with that outcome based on my fear.

Me: It makes sense but it seems like every day is a struggle to even take a shower and connect with my friends. I have nothing to live towards.

McQueen: It's because you have disconnected with yourself and your true calling. Your belonging in the Universe is lost. You have misplaced two worlds. Your sight for magic and The Great Work and also your own calling for the love of fashion. You struggled with both worlds and then you lost your business and relationship due to earthly struggles. You need to learn to let go and re-create what is truly meant to be yours. Tell me about what happened before you broke down.

My past seemed like a blur to remember. I kept it hidden because I was scared to analyze it over and over again that brought me to this point. I kept wondering what had happened? What brought me to this terrible space of suffering?

Me: The shop symbol is the sign of Ophiuchus which is my astrology sign, the 13th sign and serpent bearer. I had hired a sales guy named Sebastian due to the fact of his knowledge about the symbol and the occult.

McQueen: He was a magi reminding you of a magical past life in the occult.

Me: I had no idea about that until I put some missing pieces together. After I hired him, he came back the next day excited to give me a sketchbook with several papers of glued spells. He asked me if I remembered them because I had written them and was here for The Great Work whatever that meant. Days later, I found myself lost in the spirit world and going to graveyards late at night seeking the Inferno, seeking for the truth.

Whatever the meaning behind The Great Work was, I wasn't prepared for it then. I had no idea what it meant either. I knew minor things about the occult. I read witch spells that never made sense and never had used them because I never wanted it to come back three fold. I had many metaphysical instruments, crystal wands, smudge feathers, charms and totems. I would often burn incense and candles for prayer on my alter I created for the magnificent Godhead. Under my alter was various great books of assorted religious teachings, the Bible, the Dalai Lama, the Quran, and the lesser works of a Necromancer, the Goetia and Satanic Bible. I thought, even if I wasn't heard, the energy of it would get somewhere.

McQueen: I notice that you create paintings of that world and you are able to channel demons or malevolent spirits.

At this point, I was worried that someone would find out about my paintings and how I am able to create communication to the unknown through them. It was a gateway to other dimensions but no one knew that. If people found out, I would be deemed as crazy or disillusioned. The reasons for even channeling such evil spirits were way beyond my knowledge. I never wanted it but I had to let it happen. They wanted to communicate with me.

Me: I know that now but not in the moment and certainly have no idea how it's done. It just happens. One day I asked Sebastian to go to a grave site with me so I can get a second opinion of the spirits I was hearing. After that, everything in my life burned in gulfs of fire.

McQueen: I see that day. He never showed up and Will misread the text message thinking you were cheating on him.

Will knew Sebastian never showed up but I was hurt that he would even jump to that conclusion. Did he not have trust in me at all? Did he really think I could just jump onto someone else just like that? I couldn't believe that he would distrust me like that. I only thought of Sebastian like a brother and never even thought about the attraction between him and me. It was one of the wickedest thoughts he crept with. That I would throw our love away like that.

Me: Yes and it was havoc just knowing that he had such little trust in me. There were many things he misread that eventually ended up in my breakdown and still dealing with it now.

McQueen: But you love him so much you couldn't imagine your world without him. He will eventually find out it was all in his head one day. You two are truly meant to be. True love with extreme situations. This will somehow teach people that love isn't always perfection and it's about how you nourish it and make it grow.

Extremities was like a foundation of our relationship. One day we would be floating on air and the next he's stabbing me with emotional wounds. We had a great start the first year of our relationship. I was living life like a trophy wife, cooking and cleaning up after him making our home filled with love. He would come home from work and we just couldn't wait to see each other. He had sparks in his eyes every time we would hug returning to each other from a long day. I would make him amazing dinners and pack his lunches with colorful cut salads of five kinds of fruit, four kinds of vegetables, hard boiled eggs and cheese. Sometimes the daily salads would come with a love note saying how much I appreciated him. But this became such a foggy haze. We eventually became greedy wanting more success, a bigger home, more cars and more money.

Me: It still hurts me every day inside but he's the only one that understands me. He had this crazy idea that Carol-Lee was fused inside of me so I did see a Spiritualist to seek if it was true.

McQueen: You have always known that but couldn't explain it.

There were times when I couldn't explain that she was inside my body. She was yearning to see my father and seek how he was. It was as if she was watching him through me. There was her strong essence inside of me when I would connect with my father and every time I would go over for dinner and open a can of her favorite beer. She had a strong presence but I could never explain this to him. My father says that the dead stayed dead and I couldn't ever shake his belief.

Me: The Spiritualist did say it was true. At that point it brought me some clarity to understand some feelings I have that are not my own.

McQueen: That's why you went back home to seek and recognize pieces of yourself. You didn't like Thailand or appreciated the trip. You even stopped to journal when you got there.

If there was such thing as an old soul which I knew I had, I didn't have a connection to Thailand at all. I felt my soul didn't have a belonging there unlike places like Mexico or Cuba. At the time, I thought by getting away that I would have this deep awakening or calling to go back. I thought that the trip would be magical and I was able to view things differently or even escape my depression.

Me: I was only born there and never knew the language being thirty-five years Canadian. I met my mother's side of the family which was great but I couldn't really express myself. The part I didn't like was sitting sixteen hours on a plane and then sitting more during long drives up and down Thailand. I think I spent sixty hours in a car for the two in a half weeks I was there. All the villages and towns looked quite similar as most things they have as everything is manufactured within their own country. I did however appreciated the ancient temples as they were so alluring and magnificent. Even when the beauty of them captured my attention, I felt somewhat uncertain spiritually that my soul belonged there.

McQueen: It wasn't Thailand that bothered you. It was what you learned about your mother's side of your family and the poverty you saw emotionally. You are an Empath so you felt like to help them somehow but deep inside your heart, you couldn't. You did also see a side in fashion that threw you off.

Being in a car, unable to make the slightest exchange in communication or spending my own money by my own hand I felt trapped again. My relatives saw it as they were protecting me from harm or theft. They thought that if they treated me like a queen that I would come back to visit them. I saw that they would eat everything I wanted. My laundry was done the next day and they would sleep on the floor while I slept on a bed.

In every village I encountered, I saw the poor begging to make an exchange so they can feed their families. I saw homes that were scattered on dirt roads made out of recycled materials of metals, cement and anything they could find. Toilets that were dirt holes in the ground made me constipated as I sucked my gut in trying to find a proper release.

I felt sorrow for the Thais, I wanted to help them improve their lives like how we live in Canada. But it was hopeless. How was I going to help the humanity of the Thais live better? Could I do something of my own strength to help them? At times, I just wanted to go back home. This is not what I wanted to see. I expected to see beaches of clear waters sipping on the cold fragrant juices of coconuts.

Me: In Bangkok we went shopping in several malls and ended up in the wholesale district for garments. There were alleyways and tents set up outside with clothing bagged up on the floor and some hung up for display. I knew the garments were fresh from the manufacturers and thought about the children and poor families sewing these products. Then realized most of our garments come from places like this and felt guilty for even having to buy them. It was no longer fun to shop even though the garments were gorgeous.

McQueen: This has become a huge problem due to fast fashion. Designers know about this and how they are copied but as the population gets bigger and the companies get hungrier, we cannot slow this process down.

I have often wondered what would happen if there was a fashion collapse? What if these manufacturers couldn't produce anymore for the mainstream? Would it stop the excessive baggage that humanity carries? Would we live a more virtuous life not having fast fashion? The main extreme is that if this happened, there we would definitely see a world of the rich are richer and poor are poorer. Countries would lose contracts with trade from other countries and online buying would become more difficult. More manufacturing would be created in nations that once lost their ability to produce and the materials would become more of graded quality. But what if the Thais lost their trade in manufacturing clothing? That would mean less tourists, less money within the country and less jobs creating more poverty.

Me: The sad part is I am dirt poor and have to give into the fast fashion cycle but most of my clothes are from thrift stores as some garments are unique and some last longer.

McQueen: It certainly is in the right direction. That's why the clothing I wanted to create was high quality. I guess the real question is who can really afford it and if they can wear it a lot since fashion changes overnight? Some fashionistas are not like you. They get sick and bored of the same thing and want to express themselves in different types of dressing as life is a runway to them. The statement through my clothes was not just to see them and wear them but to have a sense of aesthetic in your own style and stick to what makes you feel uniquely powerful.

Okay, so McQueen had a point there. I was thinking this man was materialistic just because he was designing for big fashion houses and working with many celebrities. I thought this man would have a walk in closet as big as a whole floor of an apartment. I guess you would lose your aesthetic having such available garments. I think maybe he was associating aesthetic to self-expression.

Me: True to yourself I guess. That was such a good statement.

McQueen: That actually brings me back to your trip to Thailand. When you came back, you didn't even want to be associated with being Thai. It's just like your name, Apple. You have been teased and bullied because of it when it's truly part of your beauty.

Me: It was hard to see the beauty around many Thai women with bad nose jobs and dyed hair. It seemed to me they didn't even want to look Thai.

McQueen: It's within, not the outside but you seem to forget that.

I hated my name, the fact I was an Asian ethnicity and I didn't belong to a strong community where I grew up. I usually forgot that I had a nationality when I was in public. I just associated myself with just being Caucasian because it was how I was raised. My name was a big hump to get over. People often thought I named myself, Apple or assumed I was a stripper. I was teased through elementary and bullied because of my name that I ate my lunch in bathroom stalls and sat in libraries surrounded by books. I finally started using my name in public after a Fashion Stylist teacher, Tyler mentioned how beautiful it was. I reflected on it and thought yes, I guess it's created who I am meant to be. But still, I didn't want to consider myself Thai and being linked to their dysfunctions.

Me: I couldn't even seek within because I couldn't even have conversation with anybody. I was treated like a celebrity when anything I just wanted to be a tourist. My family thought that people would rob me or rip me off so they guarded me the whole trip. I didn't notice any fashionable women with their traditional dresses. It was just wrong timing since the mourning of the Thai King was still in place.

McQueen: It's like the awe you saw in the temples with examples of great artistic detail. You associated beauty seen only in features of people or race but not as Thailand as a whole. It's part of you that needs to be expressed.

I had booked my ticket the day before the Thai King had passed away. I didn't expect to go during the mourning where there was no music playing anywhere, no alcohol was served even though I don't really drink and most people were wearing all black. The country of smiles became the country of tears as they lost their country's father. They felt a doom to the age of their new King the rightful son of the throne.

Me: I guess so. The country itself was beautiful and even more because of the amazing temples that looked magical.

McQueen: It amazes me how humanity only seek beauty from the outside but not as a whole. You used to see that but you have forgotten as you pushed yourself to be part of the crowd. You are not part of the crowd, need to recognize this and except it.

I have seen myself become a tiger from the herd of sheep but have not accepted it yet. Why the gloomy thoughts and why do I feel such agony? In order to become a tiger, but why? I just wanted my happy life back. The life of when I was happy just to do laundry while humming to my own tune.

Me: But what the hell am I? Why must I be so different?

McQueen: You had a very important message directed to you over there. This was part of the reason you explored the country.

If anyone knew this, I would be deemed as crazy. It's the unimaginable to the norm. I felt like I was a monster. I don't deserve a normal human life. I just wanted to have a belonging, a place in society where I am not different.

Me: A village fortune teller told me I had been struggling with two spirits in my body fighting for my attention. One of them from the dead and the other a

spirit of a God. He told me to create a sacred space for
offerings to this God and choose just one of them
because I collected many deities. He concluded that I
was fused with the spirits of the afterlife. This was now
the fourth time hearing this and it scared the hell out of
me. He did say to let the communication flow between
me and the spirit world and that I was who I was and
that denying them I would become ill.

There was an image in my head of a friend I told, a
funny look of judgment like I was insane. I could see
everyone turning their back on me because of this
thought. It's not what I wanted to hear. I wanted to
hear great things about my future. I wanted to hear
that I would later have this amazing future with Will
with a family and making a good home surrounded by
our cherished friends. I wanted to blend into society,
the norm. But all I could visualize was their faces of
confusion and disbelief.

McQueen: Don't let others knock you down because of
this. You wanted to be normal but you are not the
norm. You are on the right path to do great things.

Me: I have not followed any God just God himself the ultimate creator.

McQueen: I hear you pray almost every day to God. There is a God within you that is able to guide and help you through your life process. It's more than a Spirit Guide, it's your protection because you have asked for it.

I heard once before that I was here to accomplish great things. I have often wondered what? I never believed that I could create or invent anything worth seeing. I never thought that anything I did was good enough. I have prayed to God almost daily even though I have believed others existed. I believe that I have a strong connection with the Godhead no matter good or evil it is. If there is a Heaven there must be a Hell. I believe that the Godhead is internally one no matter which God it is. It's the love of the belief and gathers people together in meditation, prayer or chant. I have read into the philosophy behind satanic cults and the Goetia thinking there must be living malevolent beings around us. Are they here to form against God or is it part of the Godhead to deliver messages of our dysfunctional karma?

Me: Is it bad that I seek a God within the Inferno?

McQueen: You have always asked questions about the occult. Your belief in God is grand and you have never hurt anyone intentionally and always done the right thing to please others. You have a strong Buddhist upbringing and follow his teachings. The thing that does bother you so much is by doing so much right you get hurt and misjudged so you seek spiritual protection. You know that Buddha himself does not protect you from struggling but only helps heal within and to help deal with the suffering. You are looking for a spiritual guard, something malicious and powerful.

Me: I must say that is well said. I have done so much good but I feel like I am the one that gets badly hurt and sacrifices everything for other people's happiness.

I have endured so much pain in my life that I have given up at being the angelic good girl I once was. The Noble Eightfold Path is such a beautiful concept I always had belief in and was always my inner essence but it has brought me to misery dealing with such trauma. The teachings of Christ, Islam, Hinduism and other works I understood but it would take away my independent thoughts of trying to feed the unknown. There was a truth in balancing my chakras and letting them heal but it was the same story every time I would get up piled onto other problems. The problems don't necessarily disappear, they just become bigger.

McQueen: Work on your magic. When Sebastian gave you that book he called it your Book of the Dead. You kept trying to analyze it and questioned it over time.

Me: I got scared of researching magic because I dug so deep. I discovered other Gods, Angels, Demons and lost spirits and couldn't figure out how to properly separate the entities.

McQueen: You are still on the right path. The Book of the Dead is not completed and you haven't learned yet what makes you whole. Magic is your core.

I wanted him to be right so badly. I wanted to pursue a purpose in the occult but was it right? It might open gates to the insanity or an unknown universe I couldn't escape. I had nothing to lose except sacrificing my soul to Hell if there was one. I actually was in my own Hell when I thought about it. My own selfish thoughts of abandonment, loss and heartache.

Me: But is it safe? Will God punish me or abandon me because of it?

McQueen: There is no wrong way of learning the possibilities and no wrong way of creating anything. God is forever loving and forgiving. I took my own life and he has not punished me for it. He has never left. Let me show you something I created that would help. It's called "Joan".

I wanted him to be right. I knew in my heart that God was eternal loving and forgiving. Creating my own magic would maybe help me release and obtain an outlet and heal myself. There could be consequences to dabble into such a culture.

By McQueen getting me to watch his runway shows, it was like a chore. The fashion side of me I once had was empty. I couldn't help but hear him and the messages he wanted to deliver to me. I was getting sleepy now. I cut our conversation short and stopped writing. I needed to reflect.

IV

THE SIN

I couldn't sleep all night tossing and turning until the sun light hazed over the winter sky. I couldn't help to think that there was a life for me somewhere, somewhere I truly belong. I was starting to think I wasn't supposed to be in the cycle of the mechanical 9-5 life. I was starting to think my role as a loving partner disappearing. Everything I wanted to give within myself that I once cherished has slowly wilted away.

I still burn my candles and light an incense between my fingers in prayer. I feel a welcoming breeze letting me know he was there. It was surrounding me with his loving presence. I knew that whatever I did had no wrong intention. I knew that he be right beside me cheering me on.

Depression is the number one factor that kills people every day. It has an overwhelming numbness to life that I truly understood. By looking at me no one could ever notice the scars I hid wounded inside. If there was a way to remove such a feeling I would, but I had to remove my own before theirs.

I couldn't help but reading the spells again from my Book of the Dead. Spells that I didn't really believe in them yet because they were not understood. Banishing and invoking didn't fit into my reality. I wasn't into praising or kneeling down to an idol but only have collected many charms of deities throughout the years for my alter. They have reminded me such amazing teachings throughout the history of the world. But still, even perfect teachings can secrete human kind and lead to war and decay.

I slowly lead myself back up against the futon and took out a pad and pen. As the room is filled with the smoke of myrrh, the pen started to write again.

McQueen: You're still awake.

Me: Yeah, I just couldn't sleep as I slept so much all week. My brain was wanting to work.

McQueen: It's better than being jet-lag.

Me: Anything is better than jet-lag. Mine lasted three weeks!

McQueen: Not only that but you had the anxiety of losing Will and dealing with your family issues. Also you were still struggling to know about yourself and how you fit into this world.

Old feelings of the terror of trying to sleep crept again. The mourning of loss and the heartache of each chakra flaming. Back then, I didn't understand or knew what chakras they were until I felt them heat up with anger. Each one told delivered me a message that he was having fun, being intimate with someone else while I cried my heart out day after day. The family issues were buried underneath it all and I didn't want to accept them, I didn't even except or understand myself. I was left with pieces of my identity, like my vase of only half a collection of my crow feathers left from my Alter. He took everything from me, abandoned me and was having fun with someone else while I slowly died.

Me: I have watched a video about a young man suffering from depression and was thinking how I can change it for him. I was thinking of my purpose about influencing and creating something that would help. I was looking for a sense of belonging.

McQueen: I have influenced and created but still lost myself to depression. I lost myself in the world of my own creation. My madness to explore depths where nobody has gone. The afterlife was always in my thoughts. I struggled with being alone. When I had someone to love, I didn't want it so much. I thought my love was in my career which it greatly was. My rise to fame was more of a performance, like I was the star but no one knew the real Lee. No one really got the time to dig deeply except for the people I had lost during my journey.

I knew there was a cryptic message talking to him, one can relate to such suffering. He had escaped it where I was searching for ways to heal it. It couldn't be through fashion and if so how? Fashion was part of my lifestyle I wanted to escape. It was something I blamed for five years of my life that destroyed everything I loved. I needed a vision for change I thought. I have read so many self-help books that only lead me to the same bloody place.

Me: Was there a reason for the loss of Isabella and your mother?

McQueen: Yes there was. This was to teach me the unconditional love within myself.

Unconditional love? I had to think this through. I loved myself, I mean I would never hurt myself or poison myself drinking or doing drugs to heal. I think he was trying to teach me acceptance. Inner and outer qualities. I have loved myself except for the troubles I been through. Maybe having a career and having someone to love wasn't right for me.

Me: Was this because you were so busy with your career?

McQueen: Fashion was my outlet for everything I felt inside. It was everything I was. But deep inside as a human, I was not taking care of me. Not nourishing myself. There were toxins I put into my body to help cope the stress.

Me: When Carol-Lee died, the autopsy came back with little traces of cocaine. I thought that maybe it had a huge impact on the decision to end her life.

McQueen: Cocaine was a major factor in mine. I couldn't sleep knowing I had to work the next day and then took sleeping pills. It got worse becoming addicted to other pills. It was more of a getaway for me. To take a small vacation from life and stop feeling lonely and abandoned.

Being fifteen at the time, I knew about cocaine and how it could be sniffed. It wasn't very popular to use it back then where I grew up. I just knew it was evil. When I was in my early twenties, I dabbled with cocaine at parties until I was twenty-five. I remember doing so much of it I couldn't sleep. Even worse, I couldn't afford to pay my rent. I had that feeling of regret, guilt and no way out. When I faced the mirror, I heard a voice saying "No! Not you! You cannot!" It was the first time I ever encountered something demonic even if it was trying to lead me away from the addiction.

I swelled up into tears and I prayed for forgiveness. I asked that for the exchange of staying clean if I could work for God. Then, I packed three suitcases and took the whopping $60 dollars I had left in life savings and took a ferry to the island and stayed there for four years until I was ready to come back to the city sober. That day was the last day I ever touched cocaine.

McQueen: Now when I look back, it's exactly how I wanted it. I never wanted to leave my human life but I just wanted pure happiness. I knew being a fashion robot slaving away day after day would not bring me the bliss I needed. I think you have felt the same way. You had clients that wanted more from you and you worked so hard to please everyone. You also worked on coffee and cigarettes and would forget to eat. You knew there was an end but not to my extreme. It was still a death but by saying that, a rebirth too.

Me: Yes I can relate. I did breakdown in my shop a few times thinking is this my life now? Is this what I work so hard for? To please these people? I had a happy life

learning fashion and dreaming about the possibilities.
When it became real, it became more of a headache
than a dream come true.

I had realized I was living in a fantasy world before.
How being in fashion I would have this glamorous
lifestyle. I could make people happy with designing for
their special events. Every step I took, it just wasn't
enough. Outsourcing has become a nightmare with
cheap threads and off sizes. I knew the quality wasn't
to my expectation but what was I to do when there
was a time frame? I spent hundreds of dollars tailoring
garments that should if been remade and I had clients
screaming at me so badly I would hide sobbing in the
backroom.

McQueen: I do appreciate those moments now. Even
living off of coffee and smokes. My team worked so hard
to accomplish what I needed but I became mad and
somewhat unmanageable. It was under my full control
and there was so much money involved we could do
anything with. For you it was much more a gamble. You
knew in your heart you would lose Will if you failed.

Me: I lost him and everything I owned. I had to watch him be with another woman. Even though we are trying to work things out right now, the old Will is lost. I feel like our trust is gone which was the foundation of our relationship.

It hurt me still. The loss of him. The once innocent kisses became flashes of anguish. That he could submit to someone else with the love we once had. Something that was supposed to be forever was maybe a never. I couldn't get over this. I have tried but the blistering wounds kept creeping back in.

McQueen: You love him so much you can't even give him up even if you tried. I think most of your work was the fight for true love. You two have an unconditional bond that even a huge disaster like this can't break. Even when he was with his crutch you call "his whore" you did forgive him and he did think of you every step he had with her. It felt wrong to him. You are his soul-mate dysfunctional as it sounds. No love is ever perfect but it has to bring you happiness.

Me: It's been tough. My belongings he took from me are still in storage with our ripped up memories, pictures, and sentimental cards and cherished gifts I gave him throughout the years. Everything has been torn and vandalized by him or his whore. Then I have to emotionally face pictures with him and his whore online. It's been 6 months now and finally started to heal from this trauma. I totally understand loss and heartbreak. I pity that whore because I have him back and because he was truly mine. We both have the foundation of unconditional love. I don't think at this point anything could take us away from each other. I can honestly say that it's been hard on both of us.

I had believed in soul-mates. I had believed that they endure everything together and always stayed strong and by each other's side. The reality is that he had lied to me throughout the crisis and that he was selfish not to think about what I was going through. Trying to patch things up, he still wanted a relationship that whore's kids. Where the fuck does the sacrifice end? I deeply wanted us back but not through giving that whore signals of love and affection through her children. I believe that soul-mates have an incredible bond that no one could ever take away.

I got out my laptop and gave into McQueen's request to look at Joan. Maybe there was a hidden message in there.

McQueen: It's almost the same as death. Both of you are reinventing yourselves. It's like you two had a death of an old relationship that needs rebuilding. Joan sort of reminds me of your Book of the Dead. A lot of Joan are aspects of yourself. This show was so fun to put together. It was one of my favorites.

I started watching the show and did appreciate this show more than The Doll. Each model carried attributes of myself that I didn't expect. They had gleaming red eyes that looked so beautifully stunning, something I yearned for wanting. This show was unexpected to my liking.

Me: I must say that you were ten years ahead of your time. I would wear every single piece from this show. The tailoring is impeccable and those mesh dresses say magnetically powerful. I always wanted red eyes but it's so extreme to have them and walk around here doing everyday things.

McQueen: All I can say is to be comfortable in your own skin. Don't ever give a shit about what people think, Apple. It's always been a problem for you.

Coming from an influential artist, I knew he was right. I was more worried about what people thought to be able to express myself, my true self. At the same time, I was worried about the monster I was and the scars hidden deep beneath. This show has given him sort of a light which related with the darkness in the world, and would express the beast that I felt within myself. It wasn't just the garments, it was all in the story of what McQueen was trying to tell. It was still a beautiful translation of what was in his mind. Something he needed released for humanity to see.

Me: I want to wear every single thing from this show. This is my exact styling. It's so powerful.

McQueen: Tell me what you liked.

Me: First thing I absolutely loved was your color choices.

McQueen: Shades of black and reds with tartan being the main focus on color and pattern. Red truly is your color. Being a fire sign you are drawn to it. I do dabble a lot into the mystics as well. Most of my collections have an element of the five pointed star.

I never knew he was took an interest to magic and the elements of the star. The image of Alexander McQueen's brand to me was influenced by nature. I used to see posters of his dresses with butterflies and had associated his brand with animal prints. I wasn't very educated on his designs at all. I just knew people loved his work.

Me: The fabrics you have used created that feel. That sharp energy and movement. Sheer metallic mesh, shiny malleable metal, luxurious leathers, transparent sheer, lucid knits, plush velvet's and fine wool.

McQueen: I had such a headache going through fabric choices. I wanted pure perfection. I wanted drama and every inspiration I had could if changed the fabric choice we made.

Me: The silhouettes are very classy. There wasn't so much skin shown either which is more likely what I would love to wear.

McQueen: This collection was referenced to Joan of Arc.

I really didn't know the history of Joan of Arc so I had to search it. I never learned it in school or I just never paid attention. After seconds of research, I saw that she was burned alive!

Me: Well that makes sense now! At the end of your show was a ring of fire around a model in a hooded face covered dress dancing. She was burned alive?

McQueen: Aged nineteen. Her execution was horrifying! The collection simply was influenced of her afterlife. No one really knew that I might have channeled Joan throughout the creation process. I found her to be one of the most powerful woman on Earth and that's how I wanted woman to dress like. I wanted woman to be dominant and powerful dressing in a McQueen. I wanted to carry that statement in everything I have created.

I felt sorrow for Joan of Arc and felt a strong connection to what I was feeling. At the moment of my distress, I had wrote a note expressing the feeling of burning alive. I was more flaming from the inside but from the physical body would be awfully torturous with unlimited amounts of pain. I couldn't imagine what she had to endure. I felt a whisper around me saying "You're okay". I knew I was going to be. This isn't the end. There must be some sort of passage out of this tunnel. I mean, I wasn't actually burning alive like her. This gave me hope that the flames would burn out and turn to ash.

Me: I wish I could afford anything you have created.

McQueen: It's not about having a McQueen, it's the influence I carried in my formation to empower how women dressed. You have always had that aesthetic but you felt a lot of judgment pulling it off. You need confidence and that's what my designs were recognized for. To not be afraid to step into other boundaries or the unknown. Fashion labels are not everything.

If only I had my closet again I would have pieces to my identity. I now have garments that I received second hand, a collection of leggings, tank tops and light jackets. Nothing in my wardrobe was anything interesting. I turned into someone casual to blend in with society taking the transit. My aesthetic right now was survival. Garments for staying warm in the freezing winters and cool in the sweaty summer. I didn't even have any money to buy new clothes for myself and the thought of sewing created another distraction. I was feeling irritated because I would love to express myself more fashionably. Maybe this was a sign to reinvent myself and to give up the closet that I once had and rebuild it. But would this create my happiness? Is this what I should be happy doing all my life is build myself a closet? There must be a deeper meaning to this whole conversation.

Me: I am still confused at why such a famous designer chose me to talk to and channel through.

McQueen: It's because we share many components to deliver the same messages. You understand that the spiritual realm is skin deep. My dimension has no judgment and I am also here to guide you back to what your heart truly desires.

Me: I have had a lot of struggles with the fashion industry. I refuse to be in it because I fear women a lot. Then I worked with men clients and still had to please their woman because it was more bridal.

He had to give more reasons than this. He had to give me more signals. In my heart, there was a desire for fashion long ago. The desires slowly welted away dealing with people in the industry.

McQueen: You were bullied by not only girls but boys and you had to find the reason behind it. There was no reason, it was just hardship for you to understand your true individuality. You were constantly haunted by this trauma and more so when you went back to school for Fashion Merchandising at age 30. There was a girl who befriended you and tormented you for months. She was only there to teach you a lesson.

Me: I almost dropped out of school because of her. Oh my God she gave me so much stress for months and she probably didn't even know it.

Going back to my first semester, I met a girl named Tayla. She was of Indian decent with curly dark hair and thick glasses that covered her big beautiful eyes. During my first encounters with her, I felt like I had a buddy so I started sitting in front of her. I thought she was an inspirational person. The third week of class, she ignored me for no reason. Was I not good enough as a person to not even make a friend I thought? For the rest of the gloomy winter months, I sat there alone with my back facing her. It brought me back feelings of neglect and abandonment. Just like how school was in elementary. She didn't have to say anything, I could almost hear her thoughts about me. I have done nothing to her.

McQueen: She mocked you in her head and you felt it every time. She sucked energy from weak victims around her. She needed to feel superior and when she found out how much older you were than her and your beauty at that age, it made her envious because she had to be the leader and felt lesser around you.

Me: I felt her jealous emotions at the time and I could feel my bright light go dim every time I saw her.

How could not saying nothing at all one could feel so much distress? Talya really hated me as a person. It was enough to almost quit the future in learning fashion. Maybe I should if quit then who knows. I understood that little girl inside who was bullied. It was as if it was a cycle that had to end. I wished I could help all those children that felt this way. It brought me to the story of Amanda Todd who was only fifteen when she had took her life away due to bullying. I knew she had endured such a painful experience. Bullying is such a silent sin. The intention of seeking pain and hurt of others is as painful as murdering.

McQueen: You like working independently and you are quite a hermit. That school was the best one for you to go to because you learned several lessons going there. You are beginning to close each door of the lessons you learned. Tayla was one lesson. She closed the door for bullying. You never felt safe at school spiritually but you have always loved learning. You collected every assignment and textbook as your trophy. It brought you misery every time you didn't continue with it.

Me: I never had a belonging in fashion. I felt like I wanted to lead something great at one point but I did struggle to be in the limelight. I had anxiety and problems public speaking. I had almost broke down in tears public speaking during presentations in class. I never knew what the hell was wrong with me.

The torment of trying to speak in public was the most straining thing I had to do. It was as if I was going through a mental breakdown doing it. It was taught by my parents to not speak if you're not spoken to and not speak during meals. I thought it wasn't respectful to speak for myself. I never was able to express myself through speech my whole life unless it was important to.

McQueen: You have skin issues and are very sensitive to the sun. That skin disorder made you very timid growing up. You had to face the fact of trying to fit in and even more so during the summer season not being able to show skin. You were fearful if anyone knew about your skin disorder because you thought of it being lesser and that's why you hid it so well. It actually turned you into a classy and timeless dresser.

Me: Dressing was hard as a teenager for sure. I was a bit overweight and the popular girls were just like Barbie dolls wearing miniskirts and cropped tops. They had all the boyfriends while I was too busy trying to conceal my skin.

He was right. I was never comfortable in my own skin. I was skeptical that it was from a past life but it did however make sense to me. If I can have proof of it that would tie up the karmic events. I have always been unique and always in hiding as a teenager trying to not have people observe me. It was the death of me to have someone know I was this monster underneath my clothing and even more internally.

McQueen: You have always managed to make it work. You shopped vintage and wore a lot of sheer in the summer. You were very original and that was part of the reason why you started loving fashion as a child. You had to learn to style yourself without baring skin making it trendy and unique. It builds who you are today.

The pen stopped writing and he was gone once again leaving me with my thoughts. My sister once said that without my insecurities with my skin issues I would become a stripper and lost to the world of drugs and lonely men. The thought of that scared me because I couldn't even speak in public, never mind taking off my clothes in front a bunch of strangers.

I had trouble going to beaches especially traveling where naked bodies would sun bathe on the sand. I always wished I was brave enough to tan but the thought of it made my skin itch feeling it tingly burn. I was not made for having fun in the sun like everyone else. Close friends and relatives would scratch their heads at why I covered my whole body when it was scorching hot. My excuse was that I was either living a life as a Muslim or just simply my skin was too sensitive. It made me think to myself internally that I was such a monster, not being able to be free of my body like everyone else.

I started to think about what McQueen had to say. It did however build a characteristic that I had within me. Not of myself but by having such an irritation, I always been nonjudgmental of people. My walks of shame covered with skin rashes, blotches and scars, I became humble and always looked within people. Fabrics that surrounded them never made a difference of what was really underneath. That was the confusion of fashion to me. I used fashion to hide my insecurities like a fabric mask.

I was ashamed to be naked even by myself. I would look at myself and think how could I escape this? I have been to countless doctors and used all the creams they recommended. I looked into skin bleaching and indoor tanning but that was still a scary thought. It could reverse the pigments and maybe it would become worse. I am what I am and maybe this was meant to be. It has built me to be humble, to look within people through my own disability.

V

CANDY MAN

It's been several days I have not been writing. My dreaming now has become a blurry fog since I had been taking sleeping pills that help me get through the sleepless nights. It's been a struggle tossing and turning till 5am and thought this it is it, I need my rest. I need to have some sort of peace.

I had a hazy dream last night of my uncle and grandma in a place surrounded by my youth. I saw that my grandmother was younger and my uncle was soulless floating around the home. All I gathered was being around my grandmother's old sewing machine that she carried with pride and giving her water which I would leave beside the old sewing machine.

It's the same twenty-five year old sewing machine she keeps on the foot of her bed. It's wilted with broken pieces that are patched up with tape. Her eye sight can no longer hold a vision of a needle but she still attaches herself with that possession that once filled her with joy.

She creeps out of her room about four times a day. Her frail eighty year old body is now ninety pounds. Her bottom two front teeth have broken off from a bad fall and her once full luscious head of hair has been stripping clumps bald.

I hear her twice a day caroling to Buddhist Chants which filled the home with a sense of calmness. I found it inspiring to hold such a belief, one that I should follow full time. Maybe it would help me heal or simply get away from my mind for a couple hours. What a disease, I thought to myself. I have wrapped myself into a woven blanket of worry, misery and self-pity.

If my grandmother has a way to unleash and have a sense of healing from her chanting and meditation practices, shouldn't I prepare to do this? Buddha to me was similar to Jesus. They had some remarkable teachings but I couldn't just pick either one. Both have taught me to live the right way, be kind, don't break the rules and you will receive eternal happiness. There was light in this but I still found myself wounded to the roots of human control. Going to temples and churches only made me feel segregated and isolated from free thoughts. I always thought if a person can conform into going to shrine and was content doing that, I was happy for them. It still unites to the same Godhead.

There was one thing I learned that stood out in Buddhism. One of them a saying of "this was his way of searching for enlightenment and to find your own light". I thought I had a sense of enlightenment through points of my life but they were tiny glimpses. I did see a bright light at end of the tunnel because of the extremities I had to face. I just didn't know what it would look like, I didn't even know what I wanted at this point. As I was trying to think of it, McQueen's voice came back.

McQueen: You have just received a message from an old friend.

Me: Yes, I was her friend at fifteen years old. She just let me know her brother had died from a car accident and also the old friends I had back then told her some lies about me reminded of my bullied past. Why do the people I open to trust and care hurt me?

I was reminded once again after twenty years trying to escape it. The silent sin haunts my thoughts and the daily connections I try to have with people. Scared to be back-stabbed, I often tried to stay mute. I was afraid to have a voice, not even a friend knew about how something so little can do so much damage.

I tried to bury this incident after Carol-Lee had passed away and we moved to a new home. I asked my father to take in two girls that had ran away from home. They were close to each other like cousins and I thought that by having them stay with us I would form a sense of nourishment in their company. After several months of sharing my belongings and giving them spoiled meals ordering food every day, I learned that they were both talking ill thoughts behind my back through a vent that lead to my room.

McQueen: You have a pure heart and people see that. Those girls were jealous of you and you became a martyr. You were sent here to investigate the pain and suffering of humanity. Taking on this responsibility comes with many struggles and are easily attacked because of your light. When you come back home, you will realize why you encountered your journey and who lifted you up during your struggles. You are simply, angel.

Me: I just feel like crying but it's all a weakness to humanity.

McQueen: Crying is a big part of healing pain. You will become stronger once the slivers are out. The bullying only made you hide in libraries as a child. You always felt safe with books because you had a strong connection with them. Then you would use the knowledge to unleash your own pain through writing.

My crying was so intense almost like the mourning of death. The salty tears would burn the first layer of skin and stab thorns in my heart. I couldn't be an angel, a more a demonic one likely. I always had a belief that angels stayed in the loving Ethereal. I believed that angels protect humanity from harm. Even the slightest belief of it could sound insane. Just as insane it was to talk to Ethereal beings and the late Alexander McQueen.

Me: It's the only thing that helped me cope with people. The books would talk to me providing me knowledge without judgment.

McQueen: It was an excuse to be alone and secluded because it was protecting you.

Me: I think being a loner made me connect more with the spirit world. I had to explore it to release part of myself. I felt that spirits had a place where I could relate to, a world that couldn't harm me.

Flash backs of it happened since I was five years old but one stood out more than others. I was eleven years old in a new school and there was a boy in my class that liked me. We never shared a kiss or anything like that but I had rejected him and he followed me home and kicked in my door with a couple other kids. We lived in poverty in a basement suite without any supervision or even a television. There was nothing they could even steal. All I thought was the harm of my younger brother and sister. I pushed the door with all my might to keep it from breaking while the tears ran down the slippery floor. It eventually collapsed as I was surrounded by their wicked laughter. At least they didn't come in or harm us I thought.

I tried fixing the door so that my mother didn't see, but as soon as she came home, she came after me. I had to take every hit until I gave up losing into the bruised wounds. It made me so weak to go back to school to face that boy and when I did, he had girls following me down the halls to push me around. I hid in bathrooms but there was no point, a group of girls terrorized me about my growing breasts and grabbed my boobs. I eventually pretended to go to school and ended up in public libraries surrounding myself with books that had no hurtful speech.

McQueen: It's a positive for you. There are still some deep childhood roots that burden you.

Me: My mother and father divorced when I was eleven. I have seen very bad fights where my mother was covered in blood and bruises.

McQueen: I have emotionally went through that trauma seeing a sister go through that. I was young and it was the closet of death for me. It brought me to connect with the love of appreciating the woman body and expressing their personal power through dressing them.

The images of my mother brutally beaten after a long night of her endless screams, I felt hopeless. I knew as a child it was wrong. It was horrifying but it also became the normality in my childhood. Whenever it happened, I close my eyes and vision myself to be inside a box wishing that it would turn into a world of fantasy. I wanted to desperately escape into a place that had peace, sounds of innocent laughter and golden rainbows. I understood McQueen's traumatizing experience and was impressed what he created with it. He fabricated gorgeous clothing out of something torturous look beautiful.

Me: Woman have been always suffering more pain than a man. Not saying that men don't suffer much but we endure menstrual pain, go through child birth and prone to being emotionally unstable.

McQueen: That is the reason for many of my creations to empower them. If there were no women at all, there would be less beauty and essence for life.

I wanted this to be true. I wanted to accept this but with many of the countless relationships with women where I tolerated great distress, I had blamed them for my wounds. I couldn't believe there was such wickedness in people's intentions. I read that everything in life happens because you have brought it to yourself. I heard that you have to except that responsibility that you have manifested it to you. I keep giving into the human bond with the exchange of being maliciously gossiped about. Even when there was neglect, there was a hidden silence of I wasn't worthy enough to be listened to. The thoughts of the fashion world crept up with these cruel intentions. Was this the reality of that particular industry or is a whole? If so, was there a message McQueen was trying to convey with his creativity? He simply empowered woman.

Me: But I wish sometimes to just not be able to feel, to be numb against the world.

McQueen: That's why there are so many drug addicts. They have simply got lost in their pain and found a way to hide it, try to bury it. The problem is that the issue still rises back three fold just like a magic spell.

Me: During my exploration in magic, I have never done a magic spell before. I've been a bit afraid of karmic consequences due to magic. I have always done invocations to ask for clarity and guidance and somehow it brought me to you when I was looking for something else. I desperately want to continue with magic but I am a little afraid.

I was looking for another source of the Higher Power not for God himself. Even though I would have prayer sessions, I believed God was busy and even if he didn't answer, he still heard me. I would often hear his voice saying it's okay, he's sorry, he forgives me and that he loves me.

There are often times I would be angry and not at him, at humanity. I have sought answers into the mystics, angels, demons and other Gods. It's an insane world out there and I have turned in to a monster because of it. But maybe magic would help protect me from more burden. Maybe it can guard me with a secure refuge of defense.

McQueen: This is part of your core of existence but you have lost this along the way. Society wants you to be proper and follow the rules but you were not built that way. When you rebelled the system, people were afraid of you because they have no idea what resided inside of you.

Me: Too many times it happened when I pushed the limits. Then I had to find a balance in my own lifestyle growing up. What was really right and what was wrong?

McQueen: It was through your father's job that you had to cope with trying to fit in. That's why you had dreams of fitting into the fashion industry to break the cycle. You thought you had one chance for that life to behind you.

After my mother and father divorced, I saw that he was living in a shack and I was never allowed to enter his bedroom. One day, I was curious and saw papers of white powdery substances being folded. I knew it was something bad because of the secrecy of it. I knew it was explicit, it had to be drugs.

My father started giving us money something we never had. He ended up taking on the responsibility of becoming a full-time parent with Carol-Lee by his side. We soon ended up living in a good home, indulging in good food and have a little extra spending money.

Me: Growing up with a drug dealing parent people assumed it was cool. After living such a impoverish lifestyle, it was a dream come true to be able to have a little spending money. I soon realized that I lost friends because their parents would find out even in my own small ethnic community. My father was the talk of the town and I was being punished for having such an association. He did realize that all the money in the world couldn't save the love of his life.

As soon as took her own life, we all separated from one another trying to cope with the emotional baggage. My father started to gamble everything we ever owned and had several girlfriends pregnant at the same time. I ended up with three half siblings that yearned for the emotional bond of their own father. I never blamed my father for his past mistakes or had a judgmental thoughts about his life. But when my life started to fall apart, I blamed him for the karmic consequences I had to endure. I was the closest to my father and I felt maybe there was a cryptic hidden link or a curse lingering of the suicide of Carol-Lee.

McQueen: Her spirit was revengeful towards him. There was a lot of doors that were still left open for him to close. It's been twenty years now and he will need your help to close the doors for him. He is not spiritually advanced to understand or do this. He is a young soul. She did love you more than you can imagine. She was your first inspiration to love fashion. There was something she gave you before her death that symbolizes where you are supposed to be.

The stress of trying to hide criminal activity of a parent as a teenager and dealing with the aftermath of suicide was distressing. I never knew anyone would understand my pain of trying to fit into society while this was all happening. Could anyone relate to my story? The doors have been opened for a long time.

The cycle eventually had to end somehow. Did I deserve this? Do I have to take it on?

Me: She brought me my first blazer jacket. It was pretty but very ahead of my time. Being so young, I never bothered to wear it because the cool clothes were athletics and jeans.

McQueen: I see a woman's morning tuxedo jacket.

Me: Back then I had no idea what it was called. But ya, it's kind of weird isn't it? Maybe there was a hidden message from my youth.

McQueen: There was a purpose for you at that shop. You did learn and grow.

That tuxedo jacket rang such a huge bell. It is a coincidence that I was going through a shop full of tuxedos. The thought of seeing one brought me back to feeling burned in flames. It was almost like what McQueen was portraying in his Joan fashion show. Soul-less walking models with flaring demonic eyes reminded me of my secret anger hiding inside.

Me: But what made it all tie together at to this point?

McQueen: The loop. End the cycle.

My pen stopped writing and he was gone. I had to think to myself what the loop was, how it all tied in together. I hated everything about tuxedos. I hated traditional weddings and the hardship I went through trying to fix them. I wanted to end this stupid cycle. I wanted to start releasing all this agony from my well-being. All I could think of is how fashion ruined my life.

Was there something hidden in my father's drug dealing that created this karmic event? Being the daughter of a Candy Man and lived by the life of luxury in exchange of poison. I was still associated and I have unconditional love for my father. I was his favorite, the one he mostly adored for listening to his struggles.

His greedy intentions came back. I had to distinguish the clarity beyond family. I had to separate him into two entities. The loving father and the man who fed lollipops to the diseased. I couldn't help to think that isn't the mentality ill given prescribed medications by doctors the same thing? There was a loop, there had to be an end.

He lives with his own cinema of guilty pleasures and past regret. I sometimes think he has forgotten Carol-Lee and says the dead stays dead. He would save up for months to escape to Asia to drink alcohol and be with countless women. The thought of it was reality, it was sickening to me. To try to understand a man capable of that. Especially one that has fathered many abandoned children. Each one left in the shivering cold wondering their true ancestry.

I had named my shop after my given last name, Maison Dasorine. Tuxedos came to mind again. Tailored, black wool with satin lapels. I didn't even want to picture it, they were all pieces of shattered dreams.

I needed to clear my head. I thought meditation would be good to just get some space. It wasn't going to solve the problem but my mind was starting to wonder about this loop McQueen was mentioning. I couldn't find, did it even exist?

VI

INNOCENCE

Today was a bad day. I had feelings of heartbreak all over again when I found a used condom in Will's garbage. At the time, a voice told me it's not his but I didn't listen. I just thought of the shattered dreams we shared. Memories of the charred past crept up like our ripped up pictures still laid in that cold storage room which none of us wanted to enter.

The reality was that the condom wasn't his. It was a friend of his that snuck a girl in that night. The text showed how sorry he was for sneaking her in and I was left with that guilty inner thought of being abandoned again. It was a sign of distrust.

I was scared to trust anything it wasn't even him. It was underneath my bones. I knew deep inside my soul that this love thing had to work out. It had to because

I believed so hard in it. What is life without love? It was the only positive thought in me I had left. I only craved that feeling of blissful love, nothing else mattered.

Messages flooded my phone which was the last thing I wanted. I wanted to become invisible to human interactions. I needed to gather my own thoughts about healing so I can receive the love I was devoted to. It was everything I wanted and I let it slip away. There was no one to blame but myself. Maybe I didn't deserve love anymore.

I tried burying myself in books again, staring at endless empty words. I felt as if I was selfish, secluding myself again away from human affection. I blamed only myself for this cycle of non-forgiveness and the constant insecurity of worry.

I make myself a cup of tea and my phone is buzzing. I just wanted to be alone I thought, but I gave in thinking I had to pretend I wasn't a monster. I had to except that I was part of human kind.

It didn't sound like her, she must be in distress. Her feminine mutter sounded impaired. I listened to the disturbance of her story and took it all in. I soaked up the plague of her distress and carried it on the dirt of my shoulders. It wasn't what I expected to hear. I was broken even more.

I couldn't help but to sit and reflect and try to make some peace out of it. Why do good heavyhearted people indulge in so much pain? Is this the cycle of the lifestyles of humanity? Happiness and hurt. Love and hate. Young and old. Health and sickness. Life and death. I was looking for the balance, each breath I take.

I light a candle and held the burning incense between my fingers in prayer hoping that I could find some answers. I dug my eyes into the soul-less words of my notepad wondering what it all meant. If anyone knew, I would be deemed crazy even to the insane. McQueen's presence breezed back in and I was back becoming a mutant again.

McQueen: You carry a lot of other people's emotional baggage.

Me: I don't mean to and I really don't want this. That's why I burned an incense and lit a candle and asked God to protect me against emotions that are not my own.

McQueen: Light another candle and ask to release her tension as well. You have friends that are constantly needing your advice because of your sympathetic ear without feeling judgmental. You have a trusting essence.

As the room filled with the smoke of myrrh, I knew he was right. But what was the purpose, what did it mean? I lit another candle and asked for her tension to be released. Maybe the energy of the thought can heal her worries.

Me: It's hard to say no for me. This friend has a struggling relationship with my brother. She does everything in her power to save the committed relationship they once had which he calls a friendship. She loves him so much that is hard to let go. I listened to her crippled voice today that while they were with friends having a few drinks that he insisted on a threesome. I couldn't believe how self-fish his intentions were. *With her undying love that she has for him, he was wrong to even think of that.*

McQueen: You take this on as an embarrassment to your family. Not every family is perfection.

Thinking of my family and how we are all knitted together, we always had a deep unconditional bond. I have always avoided confrontation in order to keep the peace. Try to forgive and forget past mistakes but there were clouded memories that still haunted me.

Me: He's turned into such a douche bag towards woman. Does he ever think that the karma returned could be his own blood of his niece going through the same situation? It is very hurtful and I feel the most sympathy for her. Her self-esteem for the vision for that innocent love in him has vanished.

McQueen: You see yourself in her reflection.

Me: It's as if I was going back in time again releasing that pain all over again.

The worry of failed love sunk back in and the anxiety of seeing him with another woman, kissing her lips, feeling her skin and exchanging sexual acts flooded my mind. When he says I was the one, I was the love of his life and his wife, he had proved it to be a lie.

I respectfully said nothing, I waited for him to return back to me but he was in demolished pieces. I believed in the virtue of love so much that all I could see was my illusion of a Golden Age ahead of us. I saw only pure bliss at the end of the tunnel. He was my only hope in proving true love was real. Holding our love by a thread, without him I felt I had nothing to live for. I had to prove that soul-mates exist through the extreme.

McQueen: Sex is the lowest part of how people define love. There are ways people abuse sex not only in relationships. There's a deeper meaning to this, it's in your roots. This is something you need to express so you can start to heal yourself. The last of it.

I couldn't utter any words but write. It brought me back to being mute. I know I needed to express this, something I never told a soul. Because if I did, I would be more of a monster. Even more so if people gossiped about it, and judged me for it. Even reading the forgiveness and practice of healing through the

Ho'oponopono where it teaches you to except that you brought it on yourself. This is what I brought on? This was my own fault?

Me: I was age eleven and back at that basement and the time when I was skipping school and hiding in libraries. I used to sleep in the mattress beside my sister. I remember no one was home and I was half asleep. I heard the door creek open and somebody laid between my sister and me. It was uncle by the smell of the infused stench of alcohol on his breath. I felt his hands go down my pants to underneath my underwear. I pretended I was sleeping so he didn't react and the molestation which felt like a lifetime was only ten minutes. When he stopped with me I saw that he did that to my sister for a few minutes and left the room. I felt hopeless as a child, couldn't even save myself or my little sister. I was taught to stay silent.

The thought of it made me feel numb feeling disgusted with shame and guilt. How could anyone harm a child like that? I had buried this grotesque memory in that innocent child and abandoned her. I have tried to make peace within myself for the damages but somehow this evil event came creeping back, the day I lost my sensual innocence. My eyes became flaming tears while I trying hard to hold in.

McQueen: You haven't dealt with this. You need to release it, there's lots of guilt inside.

Me: I haven't told a soul until someone at the magic bookstore mentioned it before my trip from Thailand. He mentioned it a burden that I must let go in order to receive love and pleasurable sex. He said that my love life will brighten after the wounds of it heal.

Acid teardrops landed onto the paper creating watery ink blots. Was this really the reason behind my loss of love? Was this a blockage that created my loneliness? I was scared to utter this truth to anyone. I was worried to be talked about, the scattered pieces I am.

McQueen: You are starting to close the loop soon. There's more to this, your environment has brought back to that hopeless child you once were and you feel you can't escape it.

I didn't want to explore any more stings. I was done with it now, I wanted it to be over but I knew there was one last thing to express. Maybe this would start my healing process, maybe this is the end of the loop. I was terrified to tell a soul but I had trusted this ghost. He couldn't possibly do anything to hurt me, he didn't have humanistic qualities of conviction. He wasn't going to back-stab me or gossip behind my back. I felt the security of writing it all down like I have been doing this whole time. This was the only way I could express myself being mute.

Me: My father told me a family secret before my trip to Thailand. He told me about the sexual relationship between my uncle and my grandmother. He told me that it was the reason they have always lived together.

It was all so sick, so twisted and made me the monster I am. To burden such sinful acts and repulsive, immortal behavior. I felt as if my soul was constantly being executed. My thoughts of a perfect family was hidden in dysfunctional forgiveness. The healing techniques and self-help books I hid in couldn't cure what was truly hiding inside.

McQueen: Your grandmother is sick right now and you feel obligated to take care of her because you are there.

Me: It's because I've been homeless with nowhere to go. My grandmother wasn't very influential in my life. She didn't favor me I was a child because I was dark skinned and was closer to my father. She used to make dresses for my younger sister and my uncle's daughter but not me.

My swollen eyes stopped chasing tears and I was filled with anger. I felt as though I was being combusted, flickering with gaslight. I wondered how many fucking times do I have to forgive? I saw no justice in it, I saw myself handicapped in the weakness of constant forgiving.

McQueen: She favored them for the wrong reasons. Right now I can tell you that she appreciates you being there. With that secret exposed, don't take it on but think of others that are in that same situation and ways to heal them through yourself.

Me: I am not a doctor to have authority to help people heal.

I thought I was such a monster that couldn't even heal myself to heal others. I wanted to desperately save humanity from such trials of execution. I was blazing with anger and searching for an outlet. No wonder people drink and do drugs I thought. Even if I wanted to do them, I couldn't even afford to. If I could only find an invisible drug that can numb all this shit!

McQueen: Not only doctors are allowed to heal. I want you look at my show called "Highland Rape" and examine the overall performance.

Another fucking runway show?! Fashion was the last thing I wanted to see. At this point I wanted to burn all my fashion books I kept with pride and the trophies of folders of fashion lessons. The one career I had a chance in blew up in my face and there was a dead designer communicating with me. I was already in my own insanity, nothing could shake this craziness off of me.

I still gave into McQueen's request even though I was stiff with anger. I couldn't get mad at a ghost, he was the only one I trusted with my true expression. How was this a concealed message he was trying to convey?

Me: I can see this show created lots of buzz. This show is a bit dark with lots of nudity. Theatrically, are the models raped showing your designs?

McQueen: Somewhat yes but speaking behalf of Scotland's history being the physical attribute. If you look within, it's about violence and torment within strong woman can still be overpowering. This was much more of a statement that there is beauty in darkness. Just like what you are carrying, there's such grace inside. You will never make those sinful experiences disappear but you can only form something magical from it.

I couldn't help to compare myself to every model that theatrically looked dizzy and intoxicated down the runway. It was certainly hard to watch as my insides were churning with pure hatred. Everything I loathed about my cursed experiences were walking the show. Watching the nudity, exposing strips of terror, I was unmasking through the cuts of tormented fabric. I held in my tears, it reminded me of my whole life being a rape.

Me: I almost want to cry seeing this show. It's very emotional for me. Those ripped up, shredded dresses and sheer nudity. Was this the collection that brought you clarity to what your true aesthetic in design was?

McQueen: Yes almost like glorifying the grimmest. Taking it for what it is and creating something beautiful from it creating the ultimate romance in light and dark. I never changed any horrific historical event but I used it to express parts of myself through my craft.

A romance in light and dark and a romance in joy and torment? Was this the cryptic message beyond the grave? The mind of a psychotic events fused into provocative garments of persecution. I was intrigued by his aesthetic and how he created a release for the violence of humanity with allurement. It illuminated something within me. How was he not worried of what everyone sought of the show and how was he not afraid about expressing the madness in his mind? Was this something I had to learn from him, to except the monster inside of me?

Me: It's such a bold statement and I see why you became such a sensation.

McQueen: Fame and fortune was never the intention. When you think of it, my life was like a demented fairy tale of a rags to riches gay fashion designer. I don't regret my life at all even at my death but I do miss designing for humanity.

I knew his fashion house carried on without him. I knew it would survive with the popularity of fans and fashionistas around the world. The problem was he wasn't here physically in a world where he could create woven threads into adoring clothing and keep challenging the limits. His devotion for fashion was beyond death, something I found sympathetic towards. What if he was looming over at his fashion house and not being able to speak?

Me: I can't comprehend what that would feel like to want to do something active in the lives of humanity being in another dimension without being able to be heard. It's just like me trying to find my voice to help humanity.

McQueen: You won't be able to do that depressed surrounding your thoughts of your own misery. Now you have endured such deep extremities. Think of the opposition of that. Life is death and romantically composes re-birth, it's magical.

The pen stood still and there was nothing but the calm silence. I had to reflect of what he was saying and the messages he wanted to convey. There must be a golden rainbow above the shadowy abyss, an eternal breeze of bliss behind the flaming blaze.

I couldn't help to think about the child inside me. The one I had to abandon when I was eleven as soon as her innocence was stripped away. I looked within and told her I was sorry. Seconds later, I was engulfed in weeping tears. That little girl was still inside of me yearning for me to hear her and acknowledging me she was there. While both of us sobbed in grief, I couldn't help the loop was finally near.

I had to end it for her. Her silence throughout all the tormented pain. She didn't deserve to see all this dysfunction, didn't bring on losing her innocence. I saw glimpses of the events in my life where I was mute, where she was hidden inside.

She was hiding inside school washrooms, public libraries and trying to sleep molested. She was protecting me underneath my skin making it ugly and hideous so I couldn't seduce men with it. She had to watch the aftermath of the pain of suicide, watch trade of the Candy Man and indulge into soulless paper and had to hear backstabbing through a cold vent. She pretended to adult by starting a career but was snubbed and ignored by younger competing barracudas. She constantly hid in the back room of the graveyard of used tuxedos crying about slaving to undeserving customers and a greedy mentor. She crippled to see the love of her life with someone else and everything she had left was trashed in a frozen storage locker. She was reliving the muteness everyday caring for her sick grandmother who abandoned her and plagued her with the silent shadows of incest.

I asked her to please forgive me. I never felt a cry so thunderous in my life. It was so hard that my body was trying to throw up, dry heaving air with runny

snot wiped by my sleeves. I knew I had to let it all out.
That eleven year old child I forgot in the cold needed
to be at peace.

I thanked her for both our releases. Then I heard her
say I love you. Tears once again filled my swollen eyes.
I wept away into the pillow that gave me nightmares
every night. I acknowledged the monster I was, an
angry eleven year old girl inside of me. When she lost
her innocence through trials of distrust, she stayed
burned underneath me collecting more memories of
torment.

I told her that I loved her too and the sobbing began
to stop. I was talking to my core inside, where the
unconditional love for myself was buried. Was this the
unconditional love that McQueen was supposed to
bring out in me? I was sure it was, in the depths of the
inner child. I knew perhaps if he had talked to his
inner child that he be released from his death.
Perhaps this is why some people get lost along the
way. That innocence needed to be cured in order to
move on. Maybe this was the answer to my crippling
depression and end the cycle of haunting.

I opened my Book of the Dead and wrote a poem and made a McQueen sigil beside it. I thought I need to put him to rest for now until I needed to invoke him. I heard his voice once again saying thank you. I wondered if he did release the little boy inside of him.

He has already done so much helping me release my pain. Through him I found the little demonic girl inside me, the one who experienced it all in lifeless innocent eyes. I knew that she had a fiery temper, that monster hidden deep inside.

I tossed and turned that night while hugging a teddy bear. He always looked so permanently happy and always so open for human affection. I hoped the golden rainbow was near, gathering more ideas for healing the wounds. I wanted to be an exorcist of every broken soul, fading away their worries and misery. I needed to say it's okay, I understand what's underneath.

VII

BANISH

I woke up with a phone ring and glad to hear Will's voice. Even when we are apart, it still felt we were still very near. It was the only day in about a year I felt butterflies tingle in my stomach with the heartwarming sensation running throughout my body. I was one piece again. I was no longer searching to repair myself, feeling empowered and a sense of a breakthrough. I was able to move on and leave the rest to forgiving peace.

I didn't want to think of anything else, I was happy that I had a release of my struggling pain. All the burdens of it vanished inside, just like the ashes dusting off the flames. The flicker of the candle was now a lovely, calm warming light. Staring into the beautiful essence burned away my fright.

My mother returned home that day while I was cooking grandmother's favorite tom yum soup. She explained to me that her co-worker of over fifteen years, Sandy had ghost in her home. I shrugged it off and thought, I had ghosts of my own. She explained to me that her children were scared to sleep and asked me to take a look after she was done work.

I didn't feel like doing it because I was just getting over my own problems. This was so unexpected and I was in my own selfish world where I just healed a bunch of wounds she didn't even know about. I wanted so desperately to just be alone, in my own thoughts through my own breakthrough. I had no idea what to even do about it but the fact was my mother was the only one who believed in me. She was the only one who believed that I wasn't crazy by connecting with the spirit world and their disabilities.

I agreed to have to take a look but I told her I had no idea what to do about it. I never associated myself with being a trance medium because I tried so hard to just be normal like everyone else. I never really understood or could explain what I was or how to control it. Things just happened and I couldn't stop it.

As I got ready, I thought of Sandy's children. I thought what a horrible feeling not to be able to sleep at night. Then I thought of myself as that little girl I left behind being haunted with molestation and rushed to pack my Wiccan supplies. I safely bagged a black candle that removes negativity and banishes, a myrrh incense stick, a dried bundle of white sage with my abalone shell, a smudging feather and my antler wand topped with a crystal quartz.

Walking towards my mother's restaurant two blocks away, I was thinking how the hell was I supposed to get rid of a ghost? How about if it was a demon of some sort? I thought to myself, even though if it was, come try to haunt me instead of the children because simply I had nothing to lose. I wasn't afraid of evil spirits or malevolent beings. I thought that they were all creations of a Godhead, we are all one. Like McQueen says, light in darkness just like a romantic dance.

When I got to the restaurant, I welcome myself with a hug to Sandy saying it's going to be okay. We both sat down and she explained to me what had happened. While laying down to rest in her bed, she saw a hand that looked like her teenage daughter's on the dim bathroom doorway that slowly disappeared. She went into her room and asked why she didn't answer. Her daughter replied, "Mom, I am sleeping. I didn't go to the bathroom". She said she was so confused that a hand would appear just like that.

She was terrified so she started praying to the Godhead of her Sikh religion. As soon as the recited her first two lines, a cold presence entered her sacred space and terrified her enough to continue. Minutes later, her 5 year old son rushed in her bedroom saying "Mom, I can't sleep! I am scared, please hold me to sleep!" She held her son tight that night in her bed while he slept. She explained it was the weirdest thing that ever happened to her since living in that home for six years.

I explained to her that what I would do is go into the home and light my candle and incense and ask the spirit to speak. To ask the spirit to come home with me leaving their home in the presence of peace. Then I would burn sage around the home to cleanse and clarify the ghost's presence.

I explained to her that some lost spirits can't be acknowledged by the light of God yet because sometimes they don't understand they are dead. Sometimes it might be an evil entity and will rebel against anything light or holy. I told her that I carry both the understanding love of light and darkness and that I have no judgment and come with no intentional harm.

She was happy that I came on the drive home with her because she was so terrified to have to deal with ghosts. She never believed that anything like that ever existed. I was happy to have that sense of feeling of people wanting my help. I never felt so excited about dealing with a ghost call before. It was weird to me that as soon as I let go of my burdens of my own judgment, that I was able to move forward so quickly having a sense of belonging. Is this what I was supposed to do? Is this my true calling?

As soon as I arrived inside the home, I heard a little voice saying "In the kitchen". I didn't go in that room first because I felt it would do more damage because the entity would maybe feel a threat. I walked upstairs and went to the left and sat on the living room couch. I took out my bag of occult supplies, lit my black candle and placed the incense between my fingers as I tried to communicate.

I said, "I am no harm, please come here with me and I can help you".

I sat in silence with my eyes closed as a cold breeze came in with a small voice of a non-threatening little girl. As I sat still in the stillness, she had explained she was lost. She wanted her mom, she wanted to go home. I knew the spirit didn't except the fact she was dead. I realized that she didn't understand where to go. Being that young and having lost your physical life, she must have been trying hard to get human attention for some time. I understood her, lonely in a dimension of nothingness seeking for a way out and the only thing she knew was the love of her mother.

I slipped out my abalone shell, sage and smudge feather. While burning the sage, I whisked the smoke to each corner of the room while every ash from the sage fell into the abalone shell. I asked to cleanse and clarify the space of forgiveness and peace. After having to clean the area for several minutes, I wrote a note for Sandy to recite in case the entity came back. The words read "I am sorry, please forgive me, thank you, I love you". The importance of those words from the Ho'oponopono were so powerful even my own gruesome events were vanishing and being washed away. I told her to even recite those strong words when you are afraid, in fear or even sad.

My mother soon arrived to pick me up. Sandy welcomed her inside and my mother came up the stairs and said with concern crossing her arms, "It's chilly in here!" Sandy explained to her it was a spirit of a lost little girl and that it was going to come home with you. My mother looked at me with a shocked look of terror on her face. As if it was going to now haunt us. The thought of it made me chuckle inside because she had no idea of the other entities I have connected with at home.

I explained to my mother to that we have an offering for the child and talk to her to seek what she needs. I said this spirit was not harmful at all, it was just a lost entity. My mother clarified that back in Thailand, that's what they did, it was the righteous thing to do. The thought of buying food offerings to the spirit actually made her excited that it tied into our Thai heritage, one that I used to neglect having. I soon realized to except that I am Thai with a strong English tongue and to have gratitude that I wasn't abandoned as a baby in that Thai refugee camp. I saw that by having freedom with a Canadian passport I can go anywhere in the world at any time.

Before we left the home, I mentioned to her not to worry and to let us know how she felt after we left. Sandy agreed while giving us a thank you and a warm hug. As my mother and I got into the car, she was happy that we were able to help her and that we were able to help set this spirit free.

We drove to a super market filling our basket with fruits, juices and child snacks. Then we both had a sensation of wanting a burger, something we never really ate in our home. I asked her to get some McDonald's, maybe the warm scent of a child's happy meal will seduce the spirit to have a trust in us and fill the loving hunger it needed. She agreed in faith and we quickly went to the cash register to pay for our filled basket of groceries.

Having to return home with bags of groceries, a paper bag of burgers and a boxed happy meal, we had a sense of relief that the spirit was an innocent little girl. I could hear the spirited excitement of a lost little girl wanting the pleasure of eating a happy meal. The first thing I did was open the box of the scent of fresh deep fry and a cheesy burger unwrapping the meal onto a fresh plate. I opened a container of fresh cupcakes and took one out onto the offering plate and poured a small glass of apple juice having to place it on the table beside a lit candle.

I could hear the happy little girl's enthusiasm to eat. I knew she felt safe and content with me. I knew that she was lost and looking for the affection of her mother and I knew that she didn't know she was dead.

It was as if this child was abandoned and confused between two separate dimensions.

Every time her presence came near, there was a chilly breeze. She had told me her name was Al which was short for Alana and that she was only seven years old. She let me know that she was safe with me and she was meant to be here. I was in pure joy that her spirit trusted me and happy to know that I could set her free.

Later on that night, I did a ritual of releasing her soul to the world where she belong. I asked for the light of God and his divine angels to safely guide her to the heart loving light. I couldn't wait to open my Book of the Dead to preform The Lesser Banishing Ritual of the Pentagram for our protection. I realized that maybe this is what I was, someone to understand lost souls beyond the human existence.

I was finally ready to step out in to the world again thinking that I go visit my father and my brother. I quickly got ready and packed a weekend of clothing. I texted my mother to ask if Sandy was safe. She replied yes that she was happy to have her home back. I thought what a relief to have helped her and her family. I let her know if it happened again to call me.

Right after I put the phone down, my body stoned, eyes bulging without a blink staring straight across the room at the offering plate. My whole existence knew it was filled with pure evil and hatred by the light panting. The entity possessing my body was a big one, knowing by how dense my body was and how I couldn't move. It was it... The Demonic King I had been searching for!

The possession lasted not long, only a one minute. It has been possessing me like that for decades and have no idea what his name is because it never communicates, it just watches and listens. I have no idea what it wants from me but all I know is he's not here to harm me. Because of his short visits once a year, I have been searching years through the occult about his identity. Could this be Beliel, Bune, or Bael? I have been searching to know to put him back in his rightful place to banish the harm it could be spreading.

It's a crazy thought of becoming an exorcist with both worlds of understanding life and death of the Ethereal and Inferno. Just like the beautiful romance McQueen was trying to translate for me the whole time and the gift of understanding myself, guiding towards the God within me. He made me release parts of myself I couldn't ever talk about and helped me forgive them internally. I couldn't help but to dedicate my life to help others with the same pain.

A big thank you to McQueen, as he is not only a legendary fashion designer but an influential Spirit Guide beyond dimensions teaching us fashion is not only what you wear but is also an art of expression for healing. Fashion imprints our time and delivers us messages of the past and future. I hid my imperfections in it, manipulating the world I was strong and confident wearing it and have inspired people with it at the same time. Fashion was my personal strength, it was how my friends would define me in one word. It was something I had to find again, hidden in my core.

I saw Will the same night and it was so refreshing. We had shared a night of pure bliss rekindling our future. I had learned to let things go, everyone makes mistakes and that no one including myself is perfect. Everyone is fighting their own battles and not to judge them. By the release of forgiving my inner child, I was able to unblock that invisible storm towards a healthy relationship. Something we both were originally fighting for. It was the grace of it that kept us bonded together.

He has expressed to me about taking on a teenager girl, the daughter of the whore who came between us. The whore became a bad drug addict and he saw an opportunity to save the daughter from the reoccurrence of a traumatic life. I couldn't sleep thinking all sorts of feelings of abandonment even though he doesn't have a good relationship with the mother.

In the light, I have asked for forgiveness, that love will heal us all. For me to help save her too, can help heal myself to heal others. I know she is fighting her own battles and needs a good mother figure too. So, I gave up my pride in order to help heal others no matter how much their own blood hurt me. We are all one and by accepting love for all others comes from within, it speaks volumes of what's truly inside.

I have loved this man so much that I only saw the disillusioned thought of us being together. The point is that his priority wasn't me. With all the love we shared together wasn't it enough? I was looking for my King to understand and protect me. One to not see I was a problem and keep abandoning me. I looked within myself that it's all my fault, the self-respect I had for myself shattered giving up my happiness for him. I never asked for anything in return but for us to hold each other every night. Instead he has chosen to keep our distance and us apart. So for now I will call this cold leather futon my bed waiting for my future King, the one to help complete the task of helping humanity have a golden rainbow destiny.

I had a discussion with my mother the next day. She knew I was depressed for quite some time. She had asked me about my depression while I wanted to tell her the actual truth. I had to let go twenty-five years of pain to stop the haunting misery. I told her about my uncle and that I knew about my grandmother and him then broke into wildfire tears.

My mother then consoled me and let me know she was very sorry. She let me know it had been family secret and that she was embarrassed to even talk about it, scared to have face. I let her know you have to end the cycle and that he could spread more harm to his own children. Then he would be in shame and hopefully ask for forgiveness because that ten minutes could if ruined my whole life. By sharing this, I wasn't locked up in that caged dress anymore, I was able to unleash my true potential.

Being Asian descent, they think silence is the best way. To never talk about it, it will eventually go away. The point is it will never heal and the loop continues on. So, I beg others to speak up because life is so wondrous. Don't ever let anyone take that away.

That night, I lit up my white candles and my incense to prepare for my ritual. I put on my black cloak and opened my Book of the Dead. I remember every time I do this chills run up my spine. I then recite the 3 parts of the Lesser Banishing Ritual of the Pentagram.

The first part is the acknowledgment of the Kabbalistic Cross. Staying grounded on Earth I imagine myself getting larger and larger enough so that I was big as the universe. With an enormous beam of light from the divine going through my body, I called the five parts of the cross to establish myself as the center of my universe.

The second part is tracing a large banishing star flaming of blue light and I call for the names of the enterer and feel his divine presence throughout my body with the sign of silence. I carried the white light to each four directions and recite each name with the trace of the banishing pentagram building my circle.

The last part is going back to my Kabbalistic Cross and preform the ritual of invoking the four Archangels. In front of me, Raphael. Behind me Gabriel, to my right, Michael and to my left shoulder Uriel. Then I shout "For around me shines the pentagram". I visualize a bright hexagram within my breast and shout "and within me is the six-rayed Star".

It was a magical moment of realization after the ritual. I was able to define the demonic forces and the divine. It came altogether of the reasons of my study of the Inferno, the study of Demonology, Necromancy and the Satanic. I invoked a malevolent being to understand how to put it back in the Inferno and understood how demonic possessions work.

I understood that demons house through our bodies to feed us of negatively, drown us with sickness and depression to feed the Inferno. They want our lives, they want even more, our souls. I couldn't help to think that if I perhaps never started writing and never heard McQueen that my life would be different because I saw the cycle. The tuxedo jacket given to me by Carol-Lee twenty years ago and the old tuxedo jackets that hung with sadness in my shop was supposed to be my own suicide. It was a clear message of my own death because after having one through this whole process, I became awakened.

Through my past chakra meditations and today, I finally found my Kundalini and felt it rise with white light inside of me. From there, I was no longer drowned by this humanistic life. It was what I was originally searching for my whole existence, the Goddess within me.

I am not a saint nor starting my own religion. I still live with demons daily having to see my grandmother on a daily basis. I still exchange money and indulge in good food and meat. I still drink wine when I celebrate occasions and still researching about what is truly white magic in the metaphysics. Black magic is being distributed through music, entertainment and our daily products. Without the connection of understanding the Inferno, we cannot understand the Etheral. Both worlds are connected to the creation of the New World.

The powerful word of "banish" and invoking Lilith to put the source back was now my personal tool of taking the wickedness out of my body. I can feel it there and it coming through. I understood the visits and my past nightmares being awoken with a demon fused in my body. There were things I couldn't explain in my past, flying dishes and the breaking of glass. My visit to the Guadalupe in Mexico where I received a message from the divine and the hungry demon who haunted my hotel room afterward. I knew that, the veil was opening but where there is evil there is also so much good too. The Great Work was coming together.

The Golden Age is coming near. Where lands of poverty will be at peace, the silent sin of our youth will be banished, Candy Men will fight evil and the disease of drugs will rot. We will be able to heal each other without a doctor or prescriptions. Taking away innocence and incest will no longer exist because the power of such demons will be lost and those predators will be vanished. Suicide will only exist to the purely evil who can't be in the light. All religions will be respected as one unity of the understanding of pure love of the amazing Godhead. Only the pure human kind of the light will be telepathic as the veil is opening and all will understand the worlds of the dimensions. All is beautiful, all will be one where human kind will understand the works of the Inferno and Etheral and use it with no harm. Because at the end of it all, both worlds will arrange peace but the truly wicked and evil will cease.

Later that night, I felt a breeze again, and the voice of McQueen. He says "Watch your favorite fashion show, Plato Atlantis."

I wondered how he ever knew this. This show was something I used to escape watching during school. I thought of it as fashion's future, true fashion evolution. It was the last show McQueen ever did till the end. The finale show of his escapism where reality met all the worlds. It was the most amazing show I ever saw on the runway, nothing I saw in everyone else.

Being the monster I am, I have now accepted the trials in my life I've endured that lead me to this point. If it wasn't for those feelings of pure torture and to purify them, I wouldn't grow to understand what I was now and what's to come. I didn't even have a sense I was lonely anymore even though I am alone a lot. I was being loved by my own invisible drug, the magic of the exorcism of lost internal souls and setting spirits free.

There are silent Jesus's who walk among humanity. Never underestimate anyone you encounter, they could be secretly fighting evil to protect you like me.